A RAW, REAL-LIFE JOURNEY FROM
ADDICTION TO A BETTER LIFE IN RECOVERY

HOPE DEALER

DAVID STOECKER

 FREILING
PUBLISHING

Published by Freiling Publishing,
a division of Freiling Agency, LLC.

70 Main Street, Suite 23-MEC
Warrenton, VA 20186

www.FreilingPublishing.com

Library of Congress Control Number: 2019918920

ISBN 9781950948154

Printed in the United States of America

This book is dedicated to everyone that has ever lived
with a substance use disorder and the people who love them.
May you get as much hope out of reading this book as
I have gotten while writing it.

Acknowledgments

In closing, there are many people I would like to thank, but I will only put a few here for brevity's sake.

Julie Stoecker, thank you for seeing the person I was, not the person I used to be. You have walked beside me as I have discovered who I am in recovery and what being a Christian means. I can't imagine it has been easy, but you have been my rock.

Michal Stoecker, you have always been there for me. I could not have asked for a better sister. I can honestly say I would not be alive today if it were not for you. Thank you for always believing in me even when I didn't believe in myself.

Tom Stoecker, as a father, you taught me how to love unconditionally.

Gerri Emert, you had no reason to open your doors to me to give me one last chance, yet you did. Thank you, Mom!

Nate and Becca Wessley, thank you for showing me not all Christians are judgmental hypocrites. You loved me when I couldn't even love myself.

Julie Kearbey, thank you for being tenacious as a bulldog in your prayer and faith. I believe your prayers have helped me more than I could ever imagine.

Sallie Hitchcock, as my probation officer, you could send me to prison for ten years yet chose to send me to residential treatment instead. Thank you for seeing something in me. I couldn't see in myself.

David, Jr., and Addison thank you for showing me what it means to love someone more than yourself. If not for the birth of my son, I might not have been open to the help and hope I received.

Finally, I would like to thank my Creator for His love and grace I have received in abundance!

To Christen M. Jeschke, who not only encouraged me to finish writing this book but took my run-on sentences and disparate thoughts and turned them into a book that will give encouragement and hope to many people. Thank you, you do great work.

Table of Contents

Part Two

Preface

Hi, my name is David Stoecker, and I am a person in long-term recovery. What that means for me is that I have not used alcohol or other drugs since January 31st of 2009, and because of that, I am a son, father, husband, employee, friend, counselor, director, stigma killer, and hope dealer. As a child, I was abused by multiple people. This contributed to mental health issues and a twenty-plus year fight with substance use and other negative coping methods as I tried to escape from my past unsuccessfully. I tried everything that I could to stop using drugs and live a better life, but I always fell short. Then, I was able to find long-term recovery and build an amazing life by doing what EVERY SINGLE PERSON who reads this can do.

This book is about my journey: my struggles, my successes, and what I have learned along the way. This book is also about you-- we all have struggles, and I hope that in seeing my own struggles, you will be able to identify and overcome yours. Whether it is depression, anxiety, PTSD, substance use, eating disorders, anger, etc., we all experience periods where we are not living life well. If not addressed, each one of these will continue to get worse, progressing until we can no longer function normally. We may cope for a while. We say things like, "I am doing fine," or "I am just a social drinker," or "it's nothing that I can't handle. I can quit any time I want to." Eventually, we realize the very things we were justifying as being manageable have spiraled far beyond our control—now those hurts, habits, and hang-ups have morphed into full-blown addictions that are controlling us.

There is an old proverb that I heard for the first time at an Alcoholics Anonymous meeting that portrays it this way, "The man takes a drink, then the drink takes a drink, then the drink takes the man." At first, it may be just us taking a drink or using another drug occasionally. Over time, if not immediately, that first drink or use leads to another one, which leads to another one. Eventually, that substance takes over our lives. That is the continuum that many find themselves on. Some of you may just be starting down the pathway of addiction. You may be at a point where it has not yet become a problem. Other people may think it is problematic, but you don't really know for sure because you still think you have control over it. Some may have realized it is now controlling them instead of the other way around.

No matter where you are, this book was written for you. It is written for anyone who has endured pain, hurt, abuse, loss, or is struggling with bad habits or addictions. In other words, it is for everyone. This is for the person who is considering using either to drown the pain or to fit in. It is for the person who is using but believes they have complete control over their use. If you are living with an active substance use disorder, it is for you so you can find hope that recovery is possible. It is for the person in early recovery, wondering what to do next. It is for the person in long-term recovery, knowing there is more out there but unsure what it is. It is for the person looking for answers because they love someone who is either in recovery or using and wants to understand how and why they are living their lives the way they are.

The truth is, everybody knows someone either in long-term recovery or with an active substance use disorder. There are 23.5 million people in the United States in long-term recovery. There are another twenty-two million people in active substance abuse. That totals close to fifty million people. Each of those people on average has two parents and/or step-parents, two siblings, and at least two friends. That is a total of 350 million people, which is roughly the population of the ENTIRE United States!

That said, this is a global problem. A substance use disorder does not care about your race, economic status, or culture. Worldwide, approximately 3.55 million people die annually due to alcohol and other drugs. That is one person every nine seconds or the equivalent of the entire cities of Chicago and San Francisco being wiped out annually. This is a huge problem that needs to be continually addressed. I have found some fantastic and proven ways to lay a solid foundation for sobriety and build an amazing recovery that I share in this book.

There are a lot of books out there about recovery, so why should you read this one?

As a former therapist and a recovery leader, I have worked or interacted with thousands of people who have experienced similar struggles to my own. I have seen them mired in the depths of addiction, trauma, and depression, feeling helpless, hopeless, and miserable. As a result, I have combined my own experiences with the knowledge that I gained professionally to help craft and create tools to provide a proven path of success in order to build a better life in recovery.

Why?

I am a hope dealer who has based principles for recovery on evidenced-based practices that have helped hundreds of thousands of people! I have gone from dealing dope to dealing hope, and if someone like me can live a life of recovery, then it is indeed possible for anyone. As a hope dealer who has a passion for helping people attain great lives, I feel compelled to share this so you or your loved ones can live a better life in recovery too!

Finally, this book is about so much more than just overcoming a substance use disorder. This book is about overcoming childhood abuse and other traumatic events, it is about living with bipolar disorder, anxiety disorders, and PTSD, is about losing faith and hope, then finding them again. It is about being an everyday person who found himself in a place that he no longer wanted to be living, with a life he no longer wanted to live, and not seeing a way out. If that sounds familiar to you, then this is the book for you. If I can attain sobriety and maintain it, so can you!

I am a hope dealer who believes that healed people heal people. I wrote this book to help you find your own healing and enjoy a better life in recovery so that you too can be a hope dealer!

Prologue: Evil Exists

Chambering a round, I shoved the cold steel muzzle of my gun against the back of my girlfriend's skull. Hand-knotted in her hair, I yanked back her head as I pushed her roughly to the floor. Quivering with terror as tears streamed down her face, she begged me to stop. Apologies tumbled from her lips as she tried to reason with me to release her.

"I didn't want to tell on you. The cops pulled me over with drugs in the car and were going to put me in jail. I didn't have a choice." She pleaded with me over and over again.

I was enraged by her betrayal. I had come home from doing a "burn" with a partner—a slang term for making a batch of methamphetamine. Not expecting to be at the house for very long, I had left the meth in plain sight. Showering to attempt to remove the toxic chemicals from my body, I towel dried, exiting the bathroom to discover my house being torn apart by police officers searching for drugs. I asked what they were looking for, and I was informed that they were looking for meth. Not hidden, it hadn't been difficult for them to locate what they were targeting. My girlfriend had allowed them into the house, given them permission to search, and as a result, I found myself in jail. It was an unforgivable double-dealing act, and she needed to pay.

Banking that I would be in jail long enough for her to escape from my retaliation, she was caught off guard when I returned home to confront her after being let out after only a twenty-four-hour hold. Out of all the times I had been arrested, this was the only time I had ever gotten one and was shocked when I was released without having to see a judge or bond out. It was clear that I had been released sooner than she expected, as well. Angrily entering the house, I immediately located my gun in an undisturbed stash and wasted no time in exacting my revenge. The gun pressed tightly against the back of her head, I wanted to kill her for what she had done.

Then, time seemed to stop. As if in a slow-motion scene from a movie, I was flooded with a barrage of conflicting thoughts. Feelings that she deserved to die were challenged by the sickening realization that I did not want to be haunted by the image that death left behind. Already tortured by horrible memories that preyed upon me, her death might not be another tally that I wanted to add. Killing her would cross a line that even I feared to traverse. As a rule, I did not physically harm women, yet suddenly I found myself preparing to do much worse. I knew that once the bullet left the gun, I would never be able to take it back.

As I rapidly deliberated, I saw him. He was there, lurking, screaming at me. "Pull the trigger...you coward. Don't get scared now. You HAVE to do this."

A large, looming demonic form, his presence so black as to be devoid of all light stood jeering before me. Composed of a silhouette comprised of only jagged lines and rough edges, outlined much like the rugged finish of a saw blade—he resembled a person, yet was far from human. Always cast in shadow, his face held no visible details except for his eyes...pulsating red eyes that burned deep into me every time that he looked at me. Being held in his gaze is what I imagine could only be comparable to the terror that one must feel upon first arriving and peering into the pits of hell.

Worse than the fright of his glaring eyes was the voice of what had become known to me several years prior as My Companion. He only spoke in the most horrible screams, shrieks, and torrents of yells. His whispers oozed with rage and hate, sending chills down my spine like the sound of nails on a chalkboard.

He always urged me on toward evil, spurring me towards the vilest behavior. This time was no different. I could feel him angrily pushing me to pull the trigger even as I warred within myself. He was evil beyond anyone or anything that I have ever met, and he did not like being disobeyed. I needed to do it. I needed to kill her.

He was screeching at me, taunting me to kill her even as I began to reason aloud with him. "I can't pull the trigger. I really don't want to do this."

Assuming that I was talking to her, my girlfriend pleaded, "Then put the gun down, Desperado. I know that you don't want to shoot me."

Laughing maniacally, I pulled her head back even farther and pressed the gun harder against her scalp. "I am not talking to you," I hissed, my eyes angrily flashing from green to bright blue.

"Who are you talking to?" she fearfully cried.

"My Companion. Can't you see him standing behind me? He wants me to kill you, and part of me wants to kill you as well."

Whether he revealed himself to her or the sheer terror from the insane magnitude of my words overtook her, I will never be sure. As she looked behind me, her face froze, and her eyes went wide. Her expression revealed the most intense look of panicked horror as she began to scream. There was no more begging or pleading… no words at all, just a shrill keening sound emanating from her lips.

Part One

Chapter One:

Not Picture Perfect

I was born in a town called Devil's Lake. I can't say that I remember much of that little town, but its name seemed to brand me with a foreshadowing of my future and of the Devil's mission to drown me in destruction. When cradling me close as a tiny infant, my parents could have in no way foreseen the evil that would one day control me, the lives that I would destroy, and the army of ruination that I would one day recruit for.

I didn't live in Devil's Lake long before my parents moved our family to the town of Peoria, Illinois. Located on the banks of the Illinois River, Peoria was nestled in the heart of Illinois. My earliest memories begin there, and though scattered, some are quite pleasant. I lived there with my mom, my dad, my two siblings, and our border collie. We probably seemed like the typical all-American family.

My dad and I were always close. We loved to joke around and play together. I looked forward to activities such as playing catch in the front yard with him and my big brother Jonathan. Tossing a ball back and forth, I loved the time that we spent together. Jonathan was my half brother, but my dad treated him as if he were his own son. Younger than both of us, my sister Michal looked up to her older brothers, and we teased and picked on her affectionately as brothers do.

Not one to tinker with mechanical or shop type activities; instead, my dad loved working in the garden. He had a huge garden that he enjoyed behind the house in Peoria, and I liked to play outside, especially while he gardened. One year, I remember a huge tornado that came through and ripped up a lot of trees. I watched with excitement as they cleaned up after the storm, tossing branches into the giant wood chipper.

It was here in Peoria; I received my first bike without training wheels. Severely sick with a high fever, I had been taken to the hospital to be looked at, treated, and sent home. Later that day, my dad surprised me with something that I will never forget. Still feverish, I jumped around excitedly when my dad presented me with a new bike—a cool BMX bicycle painted a steel grey and sporting red mag wheels. I was thrilled beyond measure, and there was nothing that could have kept me from riding it. Instantly enamored with the gifted bike, I begged my parents to let me go on a short ride.

"Just let me ride to the Midas and back. Please." I pleaded and cajoled until they finally relented. Jumping on my new bike, I set out to go to the top of our block and immediately return back as I had promised.

Sun reflecting off my golden blond hair, I started to ride. Pedaling as fast as my little legs could take me, I rode up to the top of the block. As I prepared to turn around, descending back to my house, I encountered two kids. One was riding his own bike, and the other was walking. I could tell that they were admiring my new wheels.

"Can I ride your bike?" asked the child on foot as he sauntered over to me. Clutching the handlebars more tightly, I refused. Undeterred by my refusal, he shoved me off it, stealing it out from under me. Then he rode off on my new bike with his friend pedaling next to him. Dejected, I never saw the bike again. That bittersweet moment experiencing the joy of my first bike contrasted with its loss stuck with me all of these years. Although awful, that child's actions pale in comparison to my first vivid memory.

My parents were Jehovah's Witnesses and, therefore, regularly attended a nearby Kingdom Hall. A family friend and member of this local congregation would babysit me whenever my parents were out. My first real memory is of her molesting me. When she babysat, she would take the opportunity to bathe me. Instead of letting me play and splash around in the bath as a typical child would, she would intentionally use each wash as an opportunity to touch my private parts in a manner groomed to gain an arousing response. As my body naturally reacted, she would repeatedly shame me, calling me "nasty" and "disgusting."

"You are such a nasty little boy. Look at you." She would touch me and then humiliate me with her taunting.

Confused and disturbed by what was happening, I had nightmares about the situation that echoed what was occurring in reality. I would see my babysitter pointing at me, laughing, and calling me names, and then this would again repeat in my nightmares. I was distraught and ashamed of what was occurring. She never acted as if she was doing anything wrong. It was only my reaction to her repeated fondling that she indicated was wrong. I was confused by my response to her violation, so I felt that I must be doing something terrible. I couldn't control it and was overcome with shame. I knew from what she said that I must be doing something disgusting and perverse, but I was less sure about the part that she played in the matter. I blamed myself. Surely, I was wrong, and this adult that my parents trusted must be right. I must be a nasty, disgusting boy—why else would my body react this way. Confused as I was, I instinctively knew that her exploitation of me was not a common thing for most people, and the shame of this made me feel different and isolated.

My worst fears were confirmed when one morning, I overheard my mom and dad talking about an article in the paper regarding an adult inappropriately touching a child. As I strained my ears to eavesdrop on their conversation, I clearly heard my parents stating how such an act was terribly disgusting. At the time, I didn't realize that they were referring to the abhorrent behavior that the adult reprehensibly carried out upon an innocent child. Instead, I thought that they were saying that the molested child was disgusting. I had internalized my babysitters mocking to the point that I believed every repugnant word that she ever spoke about me. If I needed proof that what she had repeatedly said about me was true, then that day, I felt I had it undeniably. If my parents thought that a child who was violated by an adult was disgusting, then my babysitter must have been telling the truth.

I felt that I was a nasty little boy, and I did not want my parents to know how disgusting I was, so I held my secret turmoil and shame inside. In fact, I felt so much shame that I didn't tell anyone what happened until I was an adult in my late thirties. Even as I aged and began to understand all that had indeed happened, I was afraid of telling others—fearful that they would respond, "You had an older girl playing with you, and you are complaining?" Shame forces us to keep dangerous secrets and protects those that hurt us.

The feelings that I was nasty and disgusting internalized and made me feel as if I did not fit in with the other kids, so I withdrew. Intelligent and curious, I found an escape in reading. I poured myself into books, transporting myself far away from my own troubled world through the adventures of The Hardy Boys, Nancy Drew, and The Boxcar Children. I read so much that I would get into trouble in class for reading instead of paying attention to the lessons.

The abuse made me feel different and isolated, but so did other factors. Since my parents were Jehovah's Witnesses, I was one as well, by proxy. Due to their faith, this meant that my siblings and I could not celebrate birthdays, play sports, dress up for Halloween, or make Thanksgiving and Christmas crafts or pictures. As the only Jehovah's witness in my class, I was singled out because I was different.

Although from the outside, we may have seemed like a typical family, my home life was definitely far from ordinary. My dad worked hard, but he drank harder. He would work long twelve-hour shifts and return home to drink. He wouldn't just have a casual drink or two, he got utterly hammered every day. My dad was undoubtedly what people refer to as a functioning alcoholic. He would work and then play with my siblings and me, but that is where the functioning part ended. His relationship with my mother was not "functional" at all. He would drink and then stumble into the house, making a lot of noise, which would awaken my mother. She would rage, scream, and yell, and their usual fighting pattern would commence. It was a consistent early morning alarm clock for me.

I adored my father, but living with him was difficult. In addition to his struggle with alcohol, he was also bipolar…a genetic trait inherited from his mother. Some people with bipolar disorder, including myself, have milder or more manageable forms of this condition, but my dad's were extreme. During his highs or manic periods, he would have extreme flights of fancy to the point that he needed to be institutionalized to be stabilized.

My mom tended to react physically as a result of her ongoing frustration with my father. Sometimes in a flare of temper, my mother would begin hitting my dad repeatedly. My dad would drunkenly cry, "Why are you hitting me?" as she pummeled him. As she laid into him, the sound mimicking that of a meat tenderizer mallet pounding on a slab of beef, I would hide in my room and cry. I felt helpless as I heard my dad crying, my mom yelling, and her fists pounding. I was powerless to do anything other than wish that I could disappear, becoming anybody else, going anywhere else other than where I was. I hated myself. I hated my life. Most of the time, I also hated my family.

Chapter Two:

Left and Lied To

I was so confused by everything that was going on in my life. With no way to adequately cope with what I was feeling, my anger reflected inward. I hated the situation that I was in, but I tried to bury my churning emotions deep inside. I continued to retreat into books, but after a while, even that escape didn't seem adequate. Life felt like I was always walking on eggshells as I tried to predict the safest behavior to avoid confrontation or further chaos. Even at this young age, I began to build up the walls that I would hide behind for the next thirty years.

I also began to resent and shy away from the religious beliefs set forth by my parents because even to a child, the pretense was apparent. This hypocrisy infused their lives. My parents would fight all the way to the Kingdom Hall, where we attended church. Nearly every car ride to the church, they would yell and scream at the top of their lungs while myself, Jonathan, and Michal were an unwilling audience. They would bicker, fight, and shout while we observed anxiously from the back seat of the car. As if a switch was flipped, as soon as we reached the church parking lot, the fighting and anger would stop, and the smiles would be firmly pasted on.

Stressed from the chaotic car ride, my siblings and I would pile out of the vehicle in time to gawk at the expert level charade that unfolded before us.

"Hi, brother, beautiful day today, isn't it?" they gushed.

"Hi, sister. You are looking quite lovely today." They affected an entirely different behavior than the one that my siblings and I had been held captive by just a few minutes prior.

The small amount of faith that I had in God dwindled because of this repeated display of my parents' false façade. My parents pretended to be people they were not and would force us to act like the family we had never been while we were in public. As this behavior continued, I began to associate all people who believed in God with hypocrisy, and that was an assignation that would only grow stronger as I grew older and experienced it more often.

My parents often lied, hiding the truth of what was occurring behind closed doors. In retrospect, I realize this behavior groomed and trained me to develop into the chameleon I would later become. I was living in survival mode, but I was too young to realize it. I learned to adapt my behavior to the situation, the people, and the environment. I hated that my parents hid behind lies, and I hated the helpless way these lies made me feel. My dad drank and used pornography, and my mom, in turn, took out her anger on him and those around her through verbal, emotional, or physical abuse. They were far from perfect, yet they were determined to hide what was really happening away from the world. I don't think that they considered that even as a child, I could see and struggled with their constant denial of the chaos in our lives as they publically pretended that all was perfect.

As I grew older, I noticed my parent's lies growing too. At ten years old, my mom would lie in a way that would forever alter the course of my life.

It occurred in the first week of 5th grade. It was a 1950s day at school, and I was looking forward to it. Dressed for the day's theme, I had my hair slicked back and wore a t-shirt combined with jeans that I rolled up at the bottom to best suit the theme. I was excited to pretend to be someone other than who I was, even if it was just for the day. For this one day, I thought I would fit in with everyone at school because we would all be united in pretending to be something other than what we really were. I was so pumped for the day to begin.

My mom told my siblings and me that she would drive us to school that day, and we all piled into the car. When we arrived at school, instead of enjoying the cool 1950s day that I had been looking forward to, she told us to tell our friends goodbye. Shocked, we questioned her about what was occurring, and she told us that her mother was sick and that we all needed to visit her. She assured us that we would not be gone long.

"Tell your friends that you will see them in a week or two," she urged us. We obeyed, not knowing that, in reality, we would never see them again. That day my dad waited for us at the bus stop, just like he did every day, but we never showed up. Worried, he eventually into the house and looked in our rooms. Finding that most of our belongings were gone from our home, he figured out what had occurred.

As my dad realized what had happened, I also had a realization… my mom had lied. My grandmother, although confined to a wheelchair for as long as I can remember, was not on her sickbed at all. This was just another lie that my mom used to manipulate us into going with her.

 Apparently, my mom had gotten tired of my father's constant drinking and all the fighting. She was done with his alcoholism and bad behaviors. She had gone to the leadership of the Kingdom Hall for assistance, and they hadn't helped her, so she decided to leave him without letting him know where she was going. We didn't get to voice our feelings or tell him goodbye, she just dragged us along with her. Telling us that she had to go to work in order to get us a place of our own, she deposited us along with our clothes at our grandparents' farmhouse and virtually abandoned us there. For the next year and a half, she worked two jobs. One of which included being a traveling saleswoman for a five-state region. She was gone for weeks at a time. Just like that, my parents were suddenly both pulled from my life. I felt abandoned by my parents, which in retrospect, I now know caused me to develop poor future attachment skills. Due to this, it became easy for me to destroy friendships and relationships because that is what I knew. Love was temporary, and there were no connections that couldn't be severed.

Chapter 3:

Evil Encountered

Living with my grandparents began a far more difficult period in my life, and it changed me irrevocably. From a young age, I was groomed to be a soldier of hate and destruction, and my grandfather was undoubtedly a master instructor in the terrorization of others. There had been numerous toxic guides in my early life that shaped my negative outlook and destructive behaviors, and my grandfather was one in that horrible succession.

A Navy veteran of World War II, my grandfather, Harvey, had migrated from California in the 1930s. Along with his brother, he had purchased a significant stretch of acreage near the city of Branson, Missouri, along Highway 248. His brother would eventually move back to California, leaving him the entirety of his acreage. In addition to the over one thousand acres that he owned off of the highway, he also owned another thousand plus acre property that he ran cattle on. Nestled in the heart of the Ozark Mountains, when Branson boomed, so would Harvey's property values.

My grandfather lived with my grandmother, and together they had raised their children, including my mother, on their farm.

Although wheelchair-bound, my grandmother was responsible for all the cooking, cleaning, and housekeeping. She cared for her responsibilities and didn't argue with or stand up to my grandfather. Possibly the hardest working man that I have ever known, in addition to running his own farm and bailing hay for all the neighboring farms, Harvey also worked for the Missouri Highway Department.

Life on my grandparents' farm was anything but idyllic. My grandfather was as vicious as he was hard working. In fact, Harvey was one of the cruelest, most evil people I have ever encountered. Highly volatile and extremely abusive, some mornings, he would greet us at the breakfast table by announcing his intentions to beat either my brother or me that day severely. I quickly realized that he was far from joking.

Sometimes when my dad had asked me to do something, I would teasingly refuse…prior to eventually complying. My dad was a gentle man and somewhat indulgent of my childish antics. My joking refusal was meant in good humor, and my dad knew that I was just playing around. It did not take me long to see that my grandfather was not at all similar to my dad. One day he asked me to do something, and I jokingly told him, "No," fully intending to do it immediately. His reaction caught me off guard. The opposite of the humorous response I expected, his hand whipped out and yanking me up by my hair, he dragged me to the edge of the creek. There, he cut a switch from a tree, pulled my jeans down, and began to beat me.

I shook and screamed, sobbing as he began switching me from the back of my knees all the way up to the middle of my back. He did it slowly and methodically, as I writhed underneath, crying out from the pain. He took his time terrorizing me with the switch. The chilling thing was that it was evident that he enjoyed it.

When he was done, I turned to look at him, and he had a huge smile on his face. He laughed and said, "Bet you'll never say that to me again."

As he stared at me crying, he said something I had never heard before. "That is disgusting. Boys don't cry. Stop crying, or I will give you something to cry about." Then he walked off.

I never really understood that phrase, "I will give you something to cry about." Obviously, I already had something to cry about, or I wouldn't have been in tears in the first place. To say the entire situation confused me would be an understatement. I was lost and scared, and the people that were supposed to protect and take care of me were the people that were hurting me the most.

I don't remember how soon upon arriving the physical abuse started, but it was shocking to me. My dad had never spanked me—usually letting me get away with most behavior. My mom had been the disciplinarian and she would use harsh corporal type punishment, but I had never experienced anything like this level of brutality before. The abuse was standard for my grandfather, and sadly this was just the beginning.

My grandfather's eyes were always lifeless and dull, except when he was beating my brother or me. Only then would he smile, and some of it might seep into his soulless expression. He took pleasure in regularly beating both my brother and me, routinely leaving us brutalized and battered.

My brother and I began to resent our younger sister, Michal. While we would get severely beaten, we never saw my grandfather lay a hand on her. She was Harvey's little pet, and we were jealous of the privileges bestowed upon her. It seemed that she could do no wrong in his eyes. While we would be laboring on the farm, she would get to go on early morning excursions into town with Grandpa. We envied her and would tease her about her special privileged status. Even when you are being abused, it is funny how some attention is better than no attention, and we would each vie to be chosen for special outings to town. My grandfather always chose her, and it bothered my brother and me. It wasn't until high school that I discovered that all that time, my grandfather was molesting her, often on those trips into town. We envied her for what we saw as a privilege, while my grandfather was inflicting far worse violations and abuse on her then what was done to us.

My dad loved to work in the garden, but he didn't work with more traditional tools, so I had very little knowledge of tools in general. One day I was with my grandpa in the large shop on his property, and he asked me to bring him a specific tool. My dad had never worked on cars or mechanical projects, so I didn't know what tool he was asking for. Unsure of the precise tool my grandfather was requesting, I uncertainly brought back what I guessed might be the correct tool. It was the wrong one.

"You're as worthless as your dad, aren't you?" ridiculed my grandfather. That is not the right one." I turned back to the workbench and located another tool that I thought must be it, but apparently, I was wrong again.

"Stop wasting my time," roared my grandfather as he stalked angrily towards me. "I will get it myself."

As I started to turn towards him with yet another tool grasped tightly in my hand, time seemed to skip, and the next moment I found myself face down on the concrete shop floor in a pool of my own blood. I still remember the tangy metallic taste of blood dripping down my face into my mouth.

I initially thought that he had hit me, but as the blood oozed from my face, I looked around, noting the thermos of coffee previously by my grandfather's hand was now on the floor next to me. He had violently thrown a full thermos of hot coffee directly at the back of my head, and it had knocked me out completely. I had fallen face-first onto the cold concrete, my nose and lip gashed open, bathing me in blood while I lay there unconscious.

I don't know how long I was out for, but my grandfather showed no concern. His only response to the situation was to callously tell me, "That is what you get for being an idiot. Clean your mess up and quit crying or I will give you something to cry about."

This incident was the quintessential embodiment of my grandpa. I could not even begin to recount the number of times that he hit me, kicked me, switched me, beat me, or threw something at me. He was mean through and through. Whenever he beat or abused me, he would look at me with cold, lifeless eyes and tell me that I deserved it. I thought that he must be right, and I somehow deserved his mistreatment. After all, I knew what had occurred with my babysitter. I knew that I was an unlovable, disgusting boy, and my grandfather reinforced this.

My grandmother cooked our meals and kept house—I remember her biscuits and chocolate gravy specifically. She only disciplined me one time during our entire stay at the farm. She had labored hard, making us a chocolate mayonnaise cake. The mayonnaise was used solely for moistness, and thankfully you couldn't taste it at all. All you could taste was the rich, gooey, deliciousness of a very moist chocolate cake. She had placed the cake under a bed out of the way to cool, and someone got into it. It didn't take her long to identify me as the culprit as I wore the evidence of chocolate smeared across my face. She told me that she was going to have to punish me and taking a switch, she said words that are not unfamiliar to many children and parents, "This is going to hurt me, David, more than it hurts you."

Shaking as she struggled to rise from her wheelchair, the pain of the switching really did hurt her far more than it hurt me. Switching me wracked her rheumatoid arthritis riddled body with far more pain than it inflicted on me, which oddly enough made her words come true in a very literal sense. Although this was the only time that she attempted to discipline me, her inability or lack of effort to protect us children caused me far more pain than her switching me. My grandmother knew about the abuse that my grandfather was inflicting on us. She saw it happening and was witness to the aftermath of welts, cuts, and bruises, yet she did nothing. She never once attempted to intervene, stop him, or seek help for us. I realize that she most likely lived in fear of him as well, but that didn't stop me from blaming her for her fault in the situation.

She did nothing as the abuse worsened over time. My grandfather would beat me so severely sometimes that it would be impossible to hide the evidence from it, and when that happened, he would keep me home from school for days or even a week at a time. He usually tried to keep the abuse hidden, but there were times when my face or legs would be so messed up that it would have been impossible to hide had someone truly seen me.

Often, he would call the elementary school and report to them that I was sick or that he needed my help on the farm. The school would automatically give him a pass. I felt that the school cosigned on the abuse by not ever checking up on what he was saying. He was allowed to continue to abuse me, and I figured that the school knew it, but turned a blind eye.

It was not as if I didn't try to tell someone. I did…once. It only made things worse. I had been loading wood onto the porch, but apparently was not stacking it fast enough. This was all the justification my grandfather needed to take a stick of it and split open the side of my face. When I went to school, my teacher had asked what happened, and I explained it honestly to her.

When I told her what the gash was from, the school contacted my grandfather to question him about the incident. He said to them that I was just mad at him for making me do chores and was lashing out at him by lying. He told them that we had been loading wood and that my brother had tossed a piece towards the trailer that had accidentally hit me in the face. Since this was good ole' Harvey, they never doubted the veracity of his statement.

That night my grandpa didn't punish me with a beating. Instead, he beat my brother and made me watch.

"You open your mouth again; he will get it even worse." He threatened. I believed that he would absolutely do this, so I never said another word. He even threatened to kill my mom and dad if

I said anything to them, so I stayed silent. I guarded yet another deep, shameful secret.

I fully believed then (and still do) that my grandfather would have killed my brother, sister, or parents just to spite me. He was evil, angry, and ruthlessly cruel. As a wealthy member of the good ole' boy system in Taney County, Missouri, he was well established in the community he lived in, and as a result, he was always believed. He had property and money, which helped him to appear as highly respectable in the eyes of others. No one could ever fathom the things that he did to us, nor would they have believed us over him. This scared me so much. I thought that he could get away with anything...and he did.

Completely helpless to stop him, it was during this time that I started having severe nightmares. My brother and I slept in the attic. There was only one bathroom in the house, located all the way downstairs and at the back of the house. I often woke up in that bathroom following my nightmares, scared and confused, with no precise idea of how I had gotten there.

My bad dreams were really just one constant nightmare that plagued me repeatedly as I slept. In the recurring dream, I would lose my grandfather's horse, and my grandfather would angrily chase me as I ran through the barn and into the woods to hide. I would run until I was exhausted and on the verge of collapse. Sobbing, I would hide behind a tree, all the while hearing my grandfather yelling, "I'm gonna kill you if I catch you."

As I would hear the footsteps of my grandfather nearing the tree, I would awaken, gasping, and quivering. With a start, I would find myself crying, curled up in a fetal position, in the tiny space between the toilet and bathtub.

Chapter 4:

Branson Bully

Branson, Missouri, in the early 1980s was far from the popular Midwestern mecca that now brings in over seven million tourists annually. Just beginning to open its founding theaters that would one day pull visitors from all across the country, it was still primarily a rural farming community with a population in the low two thousand.

My grandfather, Harvey, was a man of esteem in this small community. Wealth bought respect, and he had enough money and land to garner reverence among his peers in the local area. After decades of living there, he was a familiar figure to his neighbors, who thought that he was above reproach.

Obviously, this was a façade for the evil that lurked within him, yet only my siblings and I saw the truth behind the scenes. This duality in his personality made life at his farm miserable, but at school, it wasn't much better. My grandfather may have been a community insider, but I was definitely an outsider. Many of the families that I went to school with had roots going back in the community for generations. The kids all seemed to come from traditional families, wear nice clothes, and have all the coolest school accouterments such as the latest, most expensive Trapper Keepers. I had none of those things.

At least back in Peoria, some of the kids came from broken homes and didn't wear name brand clothes, but in Branson, my siblings and I were anomalies, and this was alienating. I felt alone and rejected, however, for the first time in my life, I felt another thing. I felt rage.

I wanted to be supported by the people who were supposed to be there for me. I needed to be protected by those who were supposed to protect me. I craved love from the people who were supposed to nurture me. I wished that someone would believe me or notice something was not right and would have investigated. None of that happened. Those people in my life who should have protected and nurtured me were the same people who abandoned and abused me. As time went on, I became increasingly angrier.

I assumed that no one cared what happened to me, because no one ever followed up when I told about my abuse. No one ever looked beyond the surface of my grandfather's lies or questioned why I would disappear from school for days or more at a time. These feelings flipped a switch in me. I lost hope and let in anger.

The abuse and anger that I felt as a result, profoundly changed me. Instead of fearing the pain of the abuse, I reveled in it. A masochist is someone gratified by pain, either voluntary or imposed by others, and the abuse nurtured this characteristic within me. I quickly discovered that when grandpa was in one of his moods, I could easily get him to switch me. He would start to beat me with a switch, and I would begin to laugh. My laughter would only enrage him more, and he would lose control and start hitting me with his fists. If I laughed long enough, then the payoff would be that he would wear himself out on my beating and not abuse my brother. I might also get out of school for the day, and by that time, I was ok with that. School might have initially been an escape from my grandfather, but I didn't fit in there and hated the awkward feelings that it evoked. Over time, I came to prefer missing school rather than facing an unpredictable world where I didn't belong. It may seem strange, but I gradually learned to embrace and even enjoy the pain. I especially clung to it because it had the combined effect of keeping my brother safe and keeping me out of school, where I was surrounded by kids who I felt looked down at me.

The abuse during that time also further contributed to my slow slide into agnosticism, which eventually led to atheism. I had already watched skeptically while my parents feigned faith, but now I knew that there could not be a god. If there were a god, then he would never allow me to suffer the abuse that I had been through my entire life. God was not real—and even if He was then, He couldn't possibly care about me. If God didn't care about me, then I refused to believe in or care about Him in return.

All these factors combined to fuel my rage, which burned like a furious forest fire, destroying everything in its path. No one who crossed my path was safe from the angry, irate feelings that flew forth from me. I was picked on and abused at home, and this acted as the kindling for my fury. I felt powerless, and therefore, I wanted to feel like I had some sort of power or control. To me, it seemed logical that inflicting this anger on someone else would give me the power that it would, in turn, strip from them.

It was then that I started picking on a kid who was even less popular than I was. I quickly discovered that when I picked on him, other kids would laugh, spurring me on. I didn't feel judged by the laughter, it seemed as if it was a nod towards the acceptance that I craved. So, I continued to bully. I ridiculed and picked on this kid, calling him all the names that I believed were true about myself. I would hit him when he least expected it or trip him when he wasn't paying attention. He would inevitably fall, and the other kids would laugh. Grateful that they were not laughing at or teasing me, this feeling cemented my role as a bully while in Branson.

Chapter 5:

Addicted to More

Partially through my sixth-grade year, my mother delivered on her promise to get us our own place. She had finally saved up enough to move my siblings and me out of my grandparents' home. Unfortunately, it happened to be into a house that my grandfather owned, so we still were subjected to seeing him often. He was still a constant presence, and not only that, but in the discipline department, my mother picked up where my grandfather had left off. She didn't throw things at us, but she definitely beat us with switches and violent slaps.

My first use occurred while I was living with my mom. Growing up, my mother and my father had always emphasized the dangers of smoking tobacco, yet now my mom was an active cigarette smoker. In a typical contradictory fashion, she would tell me not to smoke while harping on and on about how bad it was, then would smoke cigarettes herself. Undeterred, I began to steal her cigarettes and smoke them regularly. My mom was a traveling candy saleswoman, so we always had candy and gum available around our house. When I couldn't steal enough cigarettes, I would gather up the candy and sell it to children at my school. Using the profits from my stolen candy sales, I bought my own cigarettes from the store. Back in the 1980s, the local stores were not very strict in regards to rules involving the sale of tobacco. I could walk into any convenience store and ask to buy cigarettes for my mom, and they would let me. They had no idea that I was actually purchasing them for myself. I was only eleven years old and was already supporting an addictive habit.

When my mother left my father, he had no idea where we were located. He checked himself into rehab, and about six months later, he discovered where we were. After that, he had scheduled visitation every other weekend from Friday through Sunday. For a year and a half, he never missed a single visitation, despite living six hours away. I loved these visits with my dad, but I was too afraid of my Grandpa to use this time to tell my dad about the abuse. I knew in my heart that if I did, my grandfather would follow through on his threat to kill one of us.

When I was twelve, my father threatened to take my mom to court to gain custody of me. Before hiring a lawyer to fight it, my mother asked me which parent I would choose given the situation. I told her that I would tell the courts that I would prefer to live with my dad, so instead of fighting it, she let me go to live with him.

When he regained custody of me, my father was living in Highland, Illinois. It was a small town, not too far from St. Louis. When I lived with my grandfather, we were isolated on his farm, far from other kids. At my mom's house, there was only one child my age nearby. In Highland, I lived in a neighborhood with multiple children my age to play with. I could just be a kid for once, and I loved it. During the day, I played games like "500" and "hotbox" with the other neighborhood children, and I had a blast.

My dad and I were close, and I relished our time together. My dad worked overnights--working while I was sleeping. He had taken off a few weeks to spend time with me when I first moved there, but that could obviously not last. He would leave for work at ten each evening, instructing me, "If you wake up and I'm not here, it is because I am at work. Go back to sleep. By the time you wake up in the morning, I will be home with breakfast."

The very first night my dad went to work, I didn't go to sleep like he had told me to. Instead, I decided to take a walk to the town square, which was about a half-mile from where we lived. As I walked toward it, I encountered another kid, and we started talking. We discovered that we were both going to be entering the seventh grade, and he learned that I was new in town. He had an older brother and said I could meet him and some of his friends at the square.

"Come with me and meet them," he said.

As we approached, the kids asked my friend a question that I have heard hundreds of times since. "Is he cool?"

Then the question was directed at me, "Are you cool?" I answered the only possible way I could.

"Yeah, I'm cool," I replied. Merely saying it made me feel that it might be true.

"Do you smoke?" They asked. By this time, I had been smoking cigarettes for a while.

"Yeah, I smoke," I confidently replied, glad that I could fit in this way. A few seconds later, I was passed a strange-looking cigarette. It looked similar to the kind that one of my Grandpa's neighbors used to smoke while working on the farm--the type that you rolled yourself.

I took a drag of it before passing it on and immediately started coughing. It was a bit rougher than the cigarettes that I was used to smoking. The next time it came around, I took it and again began coughing. I was embarrassed as I hacked and choked repeatedly.

"Are you sure you've smoked before?" my new friend's brother asked me.

"Yeah, I've been smoking cigarettes for a year now," I answered, and everyone around me started laughing. I didn't understand why they were laughing, but I joined in anyway, chuckling along with the rest of them.

"This might be a little different than a cigarette. This is a joint you are smoking," he informed me.

I wanted to fit in so badly, so I took another drag with only minimal coughing this time. I admitted, "I have never smoked a joint before, but there's a first time for everything." By the time I took my fourth drag, I didn't cough at all.

It is hard to explain, but something happened to me that night. For the first time in my life, I wasn't an outcast. I never felt like I belonged or fit in anywhere, and in that circle that night, I felt the belonging that I had always longed to feel. In fact, that night, I experienced two things that I instantly fell in love with— acceptance from a group of people and numbness towards all the abuse that I had experienced.

That joint made me feel anesthetized towards all the things that had been hurting me for so long. It was as if the abuse, shame, abandonment, and rejection all faded away with the smoke from the joint. I felt giddy, goofy, and glazed. Nothing else mattered at that moment except for laughing and having fun with my new friends. It was a fantastic feeling and one that I never wanted to let go of. I was instantly hooked on getting high because getting high allowed me to numb and escape all of the trauma I had experienced.

For the rest of the week, I met my new friends in the square. I was invited to my first party that weekend. That party birthed a weekend of firsts. That weekend was the first time I drank, the first time I got drunk, the first time I tripped acid, the first time I did Mini-Thins (over the counter ephedrine tablets that have since been banned by the FDA), the first time that I kissed a girl, and the first time that I had sex. I dove straight into a sea of addictions, and I learned a critical though destructive lesson. The more that I did of all those things, the better it felt. It did not matter if it was marijuana, alcohol, amphetamines, or sex—I was instantly hooked and only wanted more.

There was nothing else that quenched my desire for more. Nothing else mattered except getting more. I loved fitting in, feeling wanted or needed, and forgetting or feeling numb. These feelings drove my excess and allowed me to escape, which was what I wanted more than anything. The prettier that a girl I slept with was, the more worthy I felt. The higher or more drunk I became, the less I thought about my babysitter, grandfather, and parents. I was quickly drowning in the devil's lake of my desire for the unquenchable thirst for more.

Chapter 6:

Highland Highs

That summer, before seventh grade, added another experience that I desperately wanted to escape from. Thanks to my new-found methods of escape, I was able to tuck it mostly away and attempt to not think about it. There was a college kid, so not really a kid at all, that we used to get drugs and alcohol from. He was home from college for the summer, and his parents were never around, so his house was one of the party places that we frequented whenever we left the square. He always had marijuana and alcohol around. One time, I made the mistake of showing up to his house alone.

He got me drunk and super high. The room began spinning while we sat and talked, although I have no memory of what precisely we were talking about. At some point, the conversation took a turn, and he asked me if I liked it when girls went down on me.

I replied, "yes." He told me that he could do better and grabbed hold of me in an attempt to show me. I tried to get up, and he pulled me down. I pushed at him, and he punched me.

"If you don't stop moving, I will beat you until you do," he said, and I tried to put up a fight. Bloody and exhausted, I finally let him do his thing, and my body reacted like it was built to do. As I physically responded to the sex act, he paused to say, "I knew that you would like it. This would not be happening if you didn't enjoy it."

Afterward, he told me that I couldn't tell anyone. "You liked it, and everyone will know that you are gay if you tell them." This statement scared me to death. I started wondering if I actually was gay or not, drinking more to try to forget it. There was not enough liquor in the world to make me forget about it, so I found reassurance of my sexuality in having sex with a lot of girls. Over time, I found that this seemed to help.

I used women like most people used toilet paper. I would sleep with them and then toss them away. The more girls that I had sex with, the less I thought that I was gay. Most weekends, I would go to a party and make out with two or three girls, then sleep with at least one of them. I rarely even knew their names, and it didn't matter to me if it was a friend's sister or the sister of a girl I had slept with the night before. A lot of the stoner girls in our group slept around, and they all had friends and sisters that were easy targets. My thirst for more was never satisfied, and I knew that if I slept with one girl from a group, I would eventually sleep with all the girls from that group. Sometimes girls would sleep with me to get back at their boyfriends or just to prove that they had a wild side since I was part of the stoner group at school. I really didn't care what the reason was. I was just happy to oblige them. The more girls I slept with, the more I felt numb and could escape the abuse from my past. By the time I moved away from Highland at the end of eighth grade, I had slept with over fifty girls.

In addition to rampant promiscuity and substance use during my stay in Highland, I also discovered an aptitude for fighting, or at least for taking punches. My first fight took place following drinking with some guys in my group and a couple of people from out of town. One of the new guys was hitting on a girl that I was friends with. She told him, "No." and he wouldn't leave her alone. Even though at around fifteen or sixteen, he was several years older than me (I was only twelve), I challenged him and started a fight. He beat me down, but I kept fighting. He knocked me back against a table, and when I came back up, there was a bottle in my hand. I smashed it against his head, and he collapsed. My friends surrounded me, regaling me with praises about how amazing the fight had been.

The next week all my friends were still talking about it. The story of the junior higher that conquered a high school kid spread like wildfire around my school. I loved the attention, the pain, the adrenaline, and the notoriety that I earned from fighting. I instantly loved violence, and I knew that I had to have it again. It was just one additional aspect of the never-ending craving for more that had begun to consume me. Drugs, alcohol, sex, and violence helped me to escape from my problems, and they made me feel amazing. I figured, why would I deal with the miseries of life when I could just escape from them? So, I dove full force into doing just that…escaping.

In Highland, I was considered a "stoner" but I was comfortable with that. I wasn't popular outside of my friend group and rarely spent time outside of my group unless I was sleeping with someone. My friends and I were seldom invited to the parties that the jocks and preps had, but we would show up anyway, and our tough reputations would ensure that they wouldn't try to kick us out. My clique was a small group of stoners, yet we were a tight-knit group of friends. I felt loyalty and acceptance that I hadn't previously felt, and although I fought when challenged, I no longer relied on bullying to feel power as I did in Branson. I genuinely felt happy and at home with my friends in Highland, and that was a feeling that I had longed for. With them, I had a sense of belonging, and through that, I felt happiness for perhaps the first time in my life. I was sure that no group of friends would ever compare to them and the little niche that I had carved out for myself in Highland.

Chapter 7:

Preppy Problems

My dad met and married a woman named Linda, and at the close of my eighth-grade year, we moved from Highland to the much smaller town of Eldorado, Illinois. Linda was already living there with her own children. Therefore, it made sense for my dad and me to join her once they married. With a population of several thousand less than Highland, this small southern Illinois town was several hours' drive from the nearest city. I was pretty sure that I would never find the friends or the happiness that I had discovered in Highland, but surprisingly I was wrong.

In Highland, I was relatively happy with who I was. I had embraced my grungy stoner style and was content with it, but my stepmother Linda was having none of it. She said something along the lines of, "I am not sending a kid that lives in my house to school dressed like that." She then threw away all my grunge-stoner style clothes and shoes and took me on a massive shopping spree to rebuild my wardrobe. This change was not my idea. I liked who I was and how I had dressed, but I entered ninth grade with a whole new preppy style. Strangely, I found that it garnered me instant acceptance and a whole new level of popularity that I had previously never found. There is a saying that "clothes make the man," and these clothes made me look preppy in a manner that endeared me to others. In Highland, I was a known partier who no parent wanted their children to associate with, but in Eldorado, I found a new mask to hide behind. I found that clothing and popularity was a mask that made me much more desirable and presentable to parents.

Additionally, my new stepbrother, Michael, helped to boost my status as a popular kid verse the potentially rejected "new kid" or "stoner" prior persona. Michael was a junior in high school and had gone to school in Eldorado since the time he had been in Kindergarten. He and I got along really well, and he introduced me to all the friends that he partied with. Along with my new preppy style, this helped to smooth my transition into my new school system.

Soon Michael's friends became my friends, and since I hung out with a lot of upperclassmen, I became even more popular within the kids in my own grade. I partied with Michael's friends and used them to help me fill my craving for more. Through this, I found my social status rose drastically. For the first time ever, I felt like I fit in with every different clique in my school. I was mostly a prep, but I treated everyone from each group the same. I knew what it felt like to be the outcast and rejected, so I made it my personal goal to be nice to everyone and never look down on anyone. This made me more popular than I had ever been before, and I felt like I had a new niche in Eldorado that surpassed even my close-knit crew in Highland.

My niche may have changed, but my addictions did not. I was still smoking, drinking, and sleeping around. My drugs of choice during this time were alcohol, marijuana, Mini-Thins, cigarettes, sex, and violence. My lust for more was like a bottomless well, and my thirst was never quenched. Since I got along with nearly everyone at my school, I got invited to all the parties. I partied with everyone: stoners, wannabe cowboys nicknamed "goat ropers," jocks, and preps. More parties meant more fights and more girls.

During this time, I also entered into the foray of vandalism. A group of kids that I hung out with enjoyed being destructive and violent, and I eagerly joined in.

Using my chameleon-like ability to adapt to a variety of circumstances, I worked to fit in and be popular wherever I was. I wasn't solely violent and destructive, I also participated in a variety of typical school activities that contributed to my popular persona. I played basketball for several hours a day, lifted weights several days a week, was on the student council, was in school plays, and made reasonably good grades. I got along with my teachers and even placed at the state speech tournaments in both impromptu and persuasive speech events. It is interesting that even back then, when I was heavily pursuing a path of destruction, God was nurturing talents such as public speaking that I would later use for His glory.

During this time, my next-door neighbor was the chief of police, and at first, I presented myself positively enough that I got along with his family and was even good friends with his son. If you didn't delve very far past the surface, I appeared to be a well-liked, successful, and popular teen.

That said, I still had a regular pattern of behavior that I adhered to. Each morning I would leave home early to get high, and then follow that up by playing basketball. During school, I would huff rush (bottles of the inhalant drug, amyl nitrate) getting stoned again during lunch. I also made it a habit to skip class during the second lunch period to get stoned. I knew the hall monitor, and they would take my name off the tardy sheet, so I never got in trouble for it. I would sit in the study hall and would spend the entire time huffing bottles of rush to get myself high. If I were not stoned, I would use it between classes as well. After school, I would usually lift weights and get high again. Then I would go hang out at a friend's house or play ball at the basketball court. I would round out my evening by getting high for the night on my walk home. The weekends I would vary my pattern by partying, getting drunk, and sleeping with my girlfriend or girlfriends depending on the circumstances. Wash, rinse, and repeat—week after week.

Inevitably though, my home life began to suffer. My father and I had always been close, but with the start of my drug use, while we were still living in Highland, I began to push away. Having struggled with alcohol addiction in the past, my dad sensed that I was drinking a lot, but I don't think that he realized that I was also involved in drugs. Both my father and my stepmother were Jehovah's Witnesses, and their strict church rules did not mesh well with my lifestyle. I got in trouble for messing around with the daughter of one of the church elders, and I was disassociated. This meant that other Jehovah's Witnesses were not allowed to speak to me any longer. As an atheist, this wasn't an issue for me. After all, I wanted to follow my own rules, and the rules of the Jehovah's Witnesses were too restrictive for me. Even if I had believed in God, it would have been impossible to measure up, following all of their rules.

As a result of the constant tension and my rebellion against my parent's rules, I ran away from home the summer before my sophomore year of high school. I lived with a friend and his family for a few weeks then bounced to another friend's house. Before I knew it, my picture was in the paper listing me as a missing child, so I turned myself in. If I were home, it would never be long before I ran away again. As a result, I soon ended up in foster care. I spent a couple of months in several different foster homes before agreeing to move back to Highland to live with my older brother, Jonathan. Jonathan was now married and employed in a steady job working for my father. For these reasons, it was decided that I might find stability living with him and his wife. My dad now owned a successful commercial cleaning business and had hired Jonathan to clean one of his stores that just so happened to be located in my former Highland haunt. Since I loved living in Highland, I was excited to be moving back, this time bearing my new preppy persona rather than that of a stoner.

Chapter 8:

My Own Mortality

When I moved back to Highland, I was only fifteen and living with my big brother was everything that I thought it would be. My brother had an apartment a couple of blocks from the square, and I quickly transformed it into a party spot. If my dad had thought that my brother and his wife would be a stabilizing force, they underestimated how dedicated I was to chasing destructive tendencies, doing the things that made me feel good. Within two months of moving in with my brother, his wife moved out. They may have been on shaky ground as far as their relationship before I moved in, but my presence and partying didn't help.

My brother worked most nights, but as a twenty-year-old, he was ready to party whenever he was home, and he enjoyed that I had a lot of cute girls there most of the time. Even at such a young age, my womanizing was out of control. If I had a party at the house and didn't have any form of sex with at least two girls each night, then I would be disappointed.

My brother played wingman for me. We developed a system where I would take a girl to the early movie only to have my brother drive by as soon as the film was out and tell me there was an emergency and I had to leave. I would get in his car, and he would drive me around the block before dropping me off for the late-night movie where I would meet up with a different girl. Usually, I would sleep with her before heading home to a raging party where I would hook up with an older girl there. In doing this, I proved a couple of things: that people wanted me, and that I had no remote concept of what a real relationship was supposed to be. I was attached to no one.

That year, life was one big party. I had thought that I had been cool in Eldorado when I hung out with upperclassmen, but that was nothing compared to hanging out with people old enough to buy their own liquor. I had my pick of girls and could party every night without any consequences. If other kids wanted to party or be popular, I was a great connection to that world.

I still got into fights regularly, but the fights between my brother and I were epic. People would gather around to watch while my brother and I fought. I held my own against him, and because of this, I thought that what I perceived to be my status rose. Our giant throw downs happened with or without an audience, and, although violent, the fights between us were usually in good fun. Before Jonathan's wife moved out, whenever we started fighting, she would begin to shift and move around furniture and breakable items to keep it safe during our destructive rows.

I was tough and fought frequently, but that didn't mean that I always won. In fact, I experienced my first couple of losses around this time. I remember getting into a fight outside of a pizza place where everybody went to play video games. A kid was staring at my girlfriend, and I called him on it. We went outside with a circle of his friends surrounding us. I hit him as hard as I could, and he ate it, then struck me so hard I saw stars. The next time he hit me, I bounced into one of his friends. I punched his friend, and his friend jumped into the fight. They beat me unconscious, but the next day when people asked me about it, my only response was, "Well, there were two of them, what do you expect."

Unfortunately, it wasn't just losses in fights that I experienced. Once, I had some problems with a particular kid that I knew, named Shawn. Shawn and I were friends but were fighting over the same girl. We set up a specific time and place for a fight between the two of us to go down, but when it was time for the fight, he never showed up. I responded by railing about what a punk he was, calling him every bad name I could come up with, and then sleeping with the girl we were fighting over.

Later, I found out the truth of why Shawn never appeared for that fight. Unbeknownst to me, Shawn's stepdad was a real piece of work and was often violent towards both Shawn and his mother. That night his stepdad began to beat Shawn's mother severely, and Shawn intervened. His stepdad pulled a gun on him, but Shawn didn't budge. He just stood there between the gun and his mother, protecting her. His stepdad pulled the trigger. Shawn died while I was sleeping with his girlfriend.

I wish that I could say that I felt bad about it, but at the time, I did not. Instead, I started telling people that Shawn chose dying over fighting against me. This lost me some friends, but I didn't care because more than enough people still wanted to party at my place.

Highland was near the city of St. Louis. The problem with this was that there was a massive influx of heavier drugs into Highland provided by individuals who had no concern for human life. Often these drugs would be cut with other drugs or laced with substances that could cause extreme reactions, which made them especially unsafe. At that time, I tried to avoid these heavier drugs, contenting myself with my usual Mini-Thins, marijuana, alcohol, the occasional hallucinogen, and very rarely, cocaine. As the alcohol and drug use around me continued to escalate, things would eventually come to a head. One night I had invited a drug dealer I had become friends with from St. Louis to come down to party with us. He and I were shot at in a drive-by outside of my brother's apartment. Neither of us actually got hit, so we just laughed about it. The following weekend, that same friend was shot and killed in St. Louis.

On the heels of that incident, one of my best friends overdosed on Valium. He was brain-dead but kept alive on life support. I visited him on occasion, but each time I saw him, I felt my own mortality. I preferred to feel and believe I was invincible, so I saw him less and less over time.

Far from actual invincibility, I soon was in a dangerous car accident. I was riding in a car full of drinking kids, and we drove past a police car. The police officer turned his vehicle around and flipped on his lights in an attempt to pull us over. Fearful of being arrested, the driver of our car responded by punching the gas. He rolled the car on the first turn he took. A friend helped me out of the car, and I ran. Later that night, I was found passed out from a crash-induced head injury and was taken to the hospital. There I was officially diagnosed with my first concussion, although I am pretty sure that between my grandfather and fighting, I probably had a few that were never evaluated.

This accident did nothing to slow me down. I should have felt my own mortality or examined my life decisions, but I did not. However, I soon experienced something that I had never felt before…I fell in love. There was a girl named Nicole, who was originally from Texas. She had been in a bunch of trouble there, so her mother sent her to Highland to live with her aunt. Hoping to help her establish a new set of positive behaviors, her mom wanted to help her get away from everything and everyone back home. I fell for her quick and hard—it was the first time that I had ever had actual feelings for a girl beyond lust.

Her aunt knew that I was trouble, and after we had been dating for about a month, forbade her from seeing me. She kept Nicole locked up tight, like a chicken in a coop, but she would sneak out late and see me anyway. Defying her aunt was not without consequences, though, and one night when I went out to meet her, she never showed up. I had some mutual friends ask around for me to try to figure out where she had gone. Apparently, because of her relationship with me, Nicole's aunt sent her back to Texas.

When I discovered this, I was shattered. For the first time since I had left Branson at twelve years old, I had wanted something and been told, "No." I did not handle this well at all, as everywhere I went reminded me of Nicole. Given my inadequate emotional coping skills, I drowned my feelings in alcohol. One night I was drinking away her loss, and the next thing I knew, I woke up in the Intensive Care Unit (ICU) of the hospital. I was informed that I had gotten alcohol poisoning, died, and been rushed to the hospital where I had been revived. My drinking had resulted in seizures prior to me passing out. No one could wake me, so an ambulance had been called. By the time it got there, I was not breathing, and my skin had turned blue.

This scare should have been a wakeup call. Instead, upon being released from the hospital during the day, I was drunk again by that evening. This concerned my brother so much so that he decided it was no longer a good idea for me to live with him. Looking back, I think that he was worried that I was going to end up dead for good if things didn't change. He decided to return me to dad and stepmom in Eldorado.

Chapter 9:

Moving Back

I loved living in Eldorado, but that didn't mean that the transition back was an easy one. The problems that had been there when I left still existed. There remained tension with my parents, and my attitude did nothing to help contribute to peace. During my six months away, my ego and confidence had skyrocketed, and so had my criminality and partying.

The police had become aware of me—my drug use, vandalism, and partying were no longer easily hidden. My partying had gotten so out of control that I was blacking out every weekend. During the week, marijuana consumed my life, along with amphetamines in the form of Mini-Thins. On the weekends, those two would hook up with alcohol to complete my trifecta of intoxicants. Somehow, I was still popular, though, and there were always girls that wanted to sleep with me.

Moving away hadn't solved the conflict at my parent's house either. My stepmom, Linda, and I did not get along at all. She cared enough to set rules for me, and I was not having that. I would come and go from the house as I pleased, so she would try different techniques to teach me a lesson. For example, when

I was hungover, she would place speakers against the wall of the living room and blare rap music against my bedroom wall to wake me up. She cared about me, and I hated her for it. My next-door neighbor, the chief of police, was worried enough about the combination of my hatred of Linda and my destructive, volatile behavior that he advised her to put a deadbolt on her bedroom door to keep her safe from me while she slept. Even so, Linda continued to care, yet I didn't.

By the end of my junior year in high school, I would get picked up regularly by the police for vandalism or assault charges. Since I was a minor, I would slide by, only being charged with lesser community service charges. However, my mask was starting to slip, the police and teachers began to see through my preppy boy persona. Eventually, after too many run-ins, I was given the choice of either leaving town or choosing to stay and face the possibility of juvenile detention. Honestly, I wasn't sure what to do at the time. Eldorado was really the only place I considered home, and I didn't want to leave. The three years that I spent there were the best three years of my life up until that point.

As I weighed the decision, something happened to tip the scales. I fell in love for the second time in my life. This time with an amazing, beautiful, smart, and compassionate girl name, Britt. She had feelings for me, too, and I promised her that we would start dating the following year when she would be a freshman, and I was to be a senior. She was kind, caring, and came from a great home. She was everything that I wanted in a girl, but not at all what I deserved. I could imagine us being the perfect couple, but I was afraid that if we began dating that I would bring her down with my own behavior. I was worried that by dating me, she would destroy her own future. She deserved better than that. I cared about her enough that I feared for her future. My feelings for her solidified my choice to leave Eldorado and protect her by never looking back.

Chapter 10:

On The Run

I had no other options but to return to living with my mom in Branson, Missouri. I moved there the summer before my senior year in high school and was hopeful that everything would turn out okay. My brother helped me get a job with him locally, and I started to make reasonably good money. I passed the time hooking up with female tourists that were vacationing for a week at a time in Branson. I also made some good friends on the cruise circuit there. In the late 1980s and early 1990s, the cruise circuit was made up of three main local hangouts— "the hill," the railroad tracks, or the lakefront on Lake Taneycomo, a man-made lake on the White River. Most of us floated around all three of these locations. By the time I moved back to Branson, it was beginning its rise towards becoming a Midwest vacation hotspot.

I picked up my partying where I had left off in Eldorado, but I now had a job which meant money to better fund my bad decisions. I quickly forgot about Britt and filled my nights sleeping with locals or other various women that I would meet on the five-mile stretch of Branson, known as the "76 Strip." Slightly resembling the Las Vegas Strip, this small portion of Highway 76 still runs through

Branson with shops or theaters scattered on either side. I would work by day, then party at night. It felt amazing.

Status was still important to me, especially on my return to a place where I had left at the lowest spot on the totem pole. Returning as the "new kid," I was accepted and brought into the fold as a cool kid instead of the rejected outcast that I had been years before. I continued to party with anyone and everyone, but here my reputation with other parents hadn't yet been tarnished, and I was able to fool them into thinking that I was a good kid.

My first summer there floated by in a haze of drunken partying. We had keg parties every night during the summer and every weekend during the school year. We would party in all the surrounding local towns—Blue Eye, Forsyth, Reed Springs, Hollister, and all the little lake towns in between. My life was one big party that summer, and I loved every minute of it. My mom was concerned about me, but I didn't care. I spent every night that I could, drinking away what was left of my youth.

It didn't take me very long to get into trouble. One night I was down on the lakefront with some friends. We had been drinking and smoking marijuana, which led to the weed driven hunger known as "the munchies." Finding ourselves across the street from the Sammy Lane Boat Dock, we decided to walk over there and help ourselves to some chips, candy bars, and a couple of pirate costumes. Unfortunately, a police officer happened to drive by while my friends and I were involved in a sword fight dressed in full-fledged pirate regalia. Obviously guilty, I received my first criminal charges for burglary and breaking and entering.

Upon entering my senior year of high school, I chose to attend high school in the neighboring town of Hollister instead of in Branson. Looking back, I am not sure how or why I made that choice, but I am glad that I did. I met a lot of amazing kids at that school. However, no matter how good the kids were that I hung out with during the school day, after school, I still sought out the party crowd. I continued to attend keg parties every weekend, which ended up being problematic. During the very first quarter of my senior year of high school, I once again had alcohol poisoning, stopped breathing, and was rushed to the hospital by ambulance, where I was admitted for several days. Hospitalized on a Saturday and released on a Thursday, by Friday night, I got drunk at another keg party. I felt like I was indestructible and in full control of my life. In reality, my addictions controlled my life and would continue to move me on a path of destruction.

During the second half of the school year, I was introduced to methamphetamines. Also known as "meth," this potent stimulant dramatically increases the amount of dopamine in the brain, which made it highly addicting. At that time, the drug's ability to be manufactured locally in a cheap but dangerous process made the drug extremely accessible. Although the manufacturing process may not have been expensive, this did not mean that the drug was cheap. With school getting in the way of partying, I dropped out of high school only a month short of graduation. Needing to fund my new meth addiction, I began stealing to get money. Between the ages of seventeen and eighteen years old, I earned additional breaking and entering and burglary felony charges.

Since I was continually getting into trouble, the court chose to send me to a psychiatrist for evaluation. I was diagnosed with bipolar disorder, generalized anxiety disorder, post-traumatic stress disorder, and antisocial personality disorder. I was also placed on house arrest and confined to my mother's house, just a block from the police station. I successfully completed house arrest with the help of friends who would sneak alcohol to me. I also would meet the occasional girl at work and was an expert at conning girls to clandestinely sneak into my house late at night to hook up with me and bring me meth, all while my mom was asleep in the house.

I spent the next year and a half on probation. During that time, I hadn't truly changed my behavior—I just became better at not getting caught. When I visited with my probation officer, he never really gave me drug screens or spent much time with me. Once I asked him, "Why do you spend twenty minutes with other people, but only a minute or two with me?

He studied me seriously and replied, "Because you are beyond repair. Why would I waste my time with you? You are going to end up in prison anyway."

It wasn't long before I fulfilled his dire prediction. Continuing my destructive habits, I was drinking and driving one night when I ran into a couple of parked cars. It was a line of taxicabs parked all in a row, and I slammed into about four of them. Drunk and afraid, I fled the scene. Initially, I thought about running away completely to Mexico or somewhere else where I could just disappear and not face up to the consequences. Once I sobered up, I turned myself in and bonded out soon after.

Just before the court case, my attorney told me that I was not going to be able to get out from under the charges associated with this incident. Scared of going to prison, I went on the run. I didn't actually leave the area. Instead, for almost a year, I worked to avoid the cops and stay out of their detection. I would bounce from couch to couch of different friends to prevent the police from linking me to a specific, consistent location that they could arrest me at. On the run, I feared being caught, but it didn't slow down or cause me to change my troubling behavior. I still partied, fought, and stole.

In fact, I would still regularly go into bars and get roaring drunk. There was one bar that I went to that had "dollar tequila night," which, in itself, is a bad idea. I always had a bit of a temper, but alcohol really brought it out. One night while drinking there, I saw a cowboy with women just dripping off him. I became irrationally jealous, seeing that he had something that I wanted, so I started a fight with him. I beat him down, and when they pulled me off of him, the bar owners threatened to call the cops and press charges. I explained to them that since I was nineteen and they had been serving alcohol all night to an under-aged minor, if they called the cops, I wouldn't be the only one getting in trouble. They refrained from calling and instead posted a picture of me behind the bar to warn their workers not to allow me in again.

Honestly, the fact that I was young when I was initially getting into so much trouble had some benefits. Even back in Highland or Eldorado, if I got into a fight and someone wanted to press charges, once they found out about my age, they would backpedal as it was often an adult in a fight with me, the minor. Assuming that I was an adult, they would want to press assault charges against me if the fight turned out bad for them as it sometimes would, but then would rapidly reverse course when they found out that they would be the one charged due to my age.

I knew that I wouldn't always be this lucky, though, and soon the meth that I used started making me paranoid. This intensified my fear of getting caught. The paranoia combined with the immense stress from worrying every minute about whether or not the police were going to find me really wore me down. Eventually, I decided just to turn myself in.

When my probation officer saw me, he asked, "What are you doing here, Mr. Stoecker?"

"I'm ready to go to prison," I replied.

"Stay seated, I'll call the county to come to get you," he ordered.

I sat there and waited as per his instructions. I stayed there until an officer from the county came and took me to the Taney County jail. Several months later, I went to the Fulton Diagnostic and Reception Center, an intake and classification center for prisoners to be processed and evaluated, located in Fulton, Missouri. There I underwent a variety of assessments and was then assigned to the location of the Boonville Correctional Facility, where I would be transported to serve my time.

Between my time in the county jail and prison, I spent about sixteen months behind bars. After dropping out of high school, just shy of earning my degree, I was able to obtain my GED while in prison at the age of twenty years old. This was probably the only positive to come out of my time there. Otherwise, my time in prison was spent learning more effective ways to commit crimes. I also got into several fights during my stay there. It was in prison where I learned that you could make pretty good money cooking and dealing meth. I had gone into prison as just a drug user, but it was there that I learned that you can make great money selling drugs. Instead of curbing my desire to avoid crime, prison helped me to hone my skills, metamorphosing me from merely a drug user into a drug dealer.

Far from reformed by my stay in prison, I got drunk on the first night of my release. Two days later, I met up with a kid that I had been introduced to while in prison who was going to help me break into the world of selling drugs. His family cooked dope, and he said that he would hook us up. When I arrived, I was told that they wouldn't have anything to do with me if I didn't shoot up on the spot. As if in a more dangerous challenge of the "are you cool?" question of my Highland days, I was given a choice to shoot up and prove that I wasn't a snitch or leave there in a body bag. If I wanted to sell, then this is what I had to do. I was sure that I wouldn't leave their shop alive if I didn't comply, so I shot up right then and there. I had only been out of prison for two days. In my naivety at just how truly evil some people out there are, I didn't even think about the risks of being hot-shotted with a lethal dose. This addition of intravenous drug use in my user arsenal only worked to speed up the already downhill progression of my life. Within a week of being out of prison, I started selling drugs for the first time using the skills and knowledge that I had gained while locked up.

Chapter 11:

Desperado

Intravenous drug use muddled my memories, making my recall of the eight years that followed both foggy and sparse. I did not do drugs for over two decades because I hated them. I loved drugs and the way that they made me feel, but I hated the person that they turned me into over time. I have heard many people say that they would not trade their worst day sober for their best day high, and I think that this statement is idiotic. My worst day sober was horrendous, and my best day high was incredible. However, that being said, I would not trade my best day sober for my best day high. Sobriety is amazing, and recovery is incredible.

Even if my recall of the events that occurred during this time were intact entirely, I would be hesitant to share all of the details. I wouldn't want my actions to be sensationalized in a way that would cause continued destruction. Sometimes within the world of substance use, there can be an almost unhealthy competition of one-upmanship or bragging that takes place reliving the glory days of drug use and that behavior is not something that I condone or want to promote.

Due to a lack of recall and responsibility, I do not have much to share during this time period. My memory from this hazy time is so mixed up that before writing this, I thought that I only had been into a detox and residential treatment stay once. As I researched my records, I was shocked to find out that I had actually been to treatment on three separate occasions.

I resumed my hard-partying ways immediately, and my drug usage continued to increase. I started staying up for a day at a time, which soon morphed into runs (periods of drug usage without sleep) of three days to weeks at a time. I slept with a ton of women as my promiscuity continued to peak. In fact, during this, I was in and out of trouble so much that in two years, I paid my attorney over $100,000 to keep me out of prison. I funded this all with the money that I made from selling drugs.

At twenty-two years old, I was drinking and driving once again when I lost control of my Firebird and went airborne. It flew ninety-seven feet, clipping trees as high as thirty-two feet up. Somehow, despite my injuries, I managed to climb to the top of a hill from the wreck site and flag a car over. I repeatedly insisted that there was another passenger in the car with me that needed to be located and treated. Soon search parties were out looking for the missing passenger using ropes to traverse the steep ravine that I had just climbed out of before collapsing. On the way to the hospital, I died three times and had to be repeatedly revived.

Meanwhile, the missing passenger was never found, and after much searching, the police concluded that I had been alone in the vehicle the entire time. My mother was convinced that the "passenger" was my guardian angel because there is no way that I should have made it out of that situation alive. In the end, I spent over a month in the hospital recovering.

Upon my release from the hospital, I had six months of chronic migraines for which I was prescribed opioids. When my prescription was stopped, I went into withdrawals, and to avoid the associated side effects, I contacted some friends to get me more pain medication. Over the next seven years, I would shoot up 100mg of morphine four times a day with my standby back up being the painkiller Dilaudid. I kept this in store for whenever my supply of morphine ran out. It was rare that my morphine ever ran out as it was not difficult to find. There was always someone who had morphine and was willing to trade it out for methamphetamine. I used morphine just to keep me from going into withdrawal, not to get high. Meth was my drug of choice for that.

The "guardian angel" passenger from my car wreck wasn't the only unknown figure that presented itself to me. A short time after beginning intravenous drug use, I began to experience the phenomena of seeing shadow people. Shadow people are figures caused by imaginings related to prolonged addiction or sleep deprivation. These figures come out of trees, from around corners, or run by you so fast that you can only catch a glimpse of their wispy forms. If you try to look directly at it, the figure fades away, blends in, or disappears completely. Your mind is unable to explain what it sees, so it rationalizes it as something understandable. An atheist, when I first saw a shadow person, I did not believe in spirits or spiritual warfare of any sort. I would tell myself that perhaps what I saw was the wind moving a branch, which triggered my imagination into thinking that I saw something that I didn't—or perhaps it was just psychosis from being awake for a week at a time. Sometimes, I became paranoid, thinking that the police were watching me, waiting to arrest me. Other people's shadow people manifest to them as imagined drug task forces or DEA agents, and it is for this reason that so many drug addicts become paranoid about being watched when they are not actually being observed by anyone.

Over time, my shadow people became a shadow person. It might be joined by other shadows if I was around other people, but only then. Some people I had talked to report seeing groups of shadow people when they were by themselves, but whenever I was alone, I just saw one shadow person.

Disconcerting as it was that this shadow person had begun to be a regular presence in my life, I had other real-life issues that were spiraling out of control.

When I was twenty-four, my sister and I were living together. One morning, I awoke to my sister, yelling at me and shaking me awake. "Where is my car?" she demanded. Disoriented and exhausted after shooting up morphine and partying all night, I had blacked out at a club the night before only to awaken to her angry voice.

"It's outside," I told her. She dragged me outside and directed me to start looking for it. We couldn't find it in the apartment complex, so we hopped in my car and headed out to look for it along the road. The night before, I had driven her car instead of mine, irrationally convinced that the cops were out looking for me and would try to identify me based on my vehicle.

As we drove, she filled me in on what had occurred while I had been passed out. She was livid. "Our neighbors woke me up this morning and asked me if you were my brother. When I replied, 'yes,' they told me to come to get you. You were in the wrong apartment. I guess you walked into their apartment, ate food out of the refrigerator, and then crashed on their couch. You are lucky they knew who you were and didn't call the cops or shoot you for being in their apartment."

She was furious with me for putting her in that position and anxious to locate her missing car. Our search had been unsuccessful up to that point, and just as she was placing her phone up to her ear to call 911 and report the car stolen, she saw it. It was completely totaled and lay upside down in a ditch off the side of the road. We were later able to piece together the facts of the previous night. Apparently, I hadn't just blacked out at a club. I had consumed alcohol until I was blackout drunk and yet, somehow, thought it was a good idea to drive home in that state. As I weaved towards my sister's apartment complex, I lost control and rolled the vehicle several times. I then ran from the wreck and into our neighbor's home, mistaking it for mine. I crashed out on their couch, thinking that I was in my own apartment until my sister woke me up the next day. Luckily the neighbors knew who I was and did not want to press charges. My report to the insurance company said that I had swerved to avoid a deer, and they believed me, so a wrecker was called and the car was towed off without the police being notified.

Around that same time, I started working at a large restaurant in Branson called Mesquite Charlie's Steakhouse. Everyone that worked there was given a call name, and mine was Desperado. I fully adopted this name for everything from work, to drug deals, to daily life. Pretty much everyone came to know me exclusively as Desperado.

While working at Mesquite Charlie's and growing my drug selling skills, a new girl came into the restaurant to work. Beautiful and from a tiny town in Arkansas, she had been raised in an extremely conservative community. She was from a very fundamental Christian background where the women in their church community wore long skirts or dresses for modesty and rarely ventured out into the world. She came into the restaurant just out of high school at the age of eighteen. The moment that I saw her, I knew that I had to have her. Her name was Olivia, call name: Santa Fe, as we all had country western sounding names to fit with the restaurant theme. We started dating, and I ended up introducing her to meth. I would work six double shifts and take Mondays off, and she would do the same, taking Tuesdays as her day off as one of the two of us usually had to be working the restaurant floor on any given day. We would do meth, staying up without sleep until it was our day off. A potent stimulant, meth use is not conducive to promoting any sort of regular sleep patterns. We would stay up together playing video games, coloring, or anything to pass the time along. Although I introduced her to meth, I would not allow her to shoot it up. In fact, I would threaten to cut people off if I ever found out that they had gotten her to shoot up.

Being that it was such a large restaurant that employed so many employees, Mesquite Charlie's had a unique feature in that they provided onsite apartments below the restaurant for their employees. This may have seemed like a good idea, but it was a horrible one. Restaurant and bar culture being as they were, employees would party hard after work, and then fights would break out late into the night. The police were called continuously to break up brawls. I sold a lot of drugs to my fellow employees that lived in these apartments. One guy that I introduced to the needle sold drugs for me, and when I broke up with my girlfriend Santa Fe, he started dating her. He, in turn, taught her to shoot up, and they would use together. They eventually married, had four children, and moved away, but never shook off the demon of drugs and addiction. I lost track of their lives until a few years later, when a mutual friend asked me if I had heard about what had happened to Olivia.

"No, what happened?" I asked.

"She and her husband caught a blood-borne infection from a needle they shared, and both died," she replied matter of factly.

"Oh wow. Did they have any kids?" I responded, stunned.

"Yeah, they left four kids behind," she answered sadly.

Throughout the years, I have kept an eye on those kids from afar. Although I didn't give her or her husband the drugs that directly killed them, I do feel the heavy burden for the part that I played in both of their addiction. That feeling of responsibility isn't something that I allow myself to let go of. I have even reached out to his brother and her sister to apologize, but have never heard back from them. Often when those of us who struggled with drug addiction become sober, we tend to glorify our drug days and only remember them in the best light. People start to get rose-colored glasses and look back fondly on their glory days of the past. I don't ever want to do that. I don't want to ever look back on those days with a greater appreciation then for the days that I am living now drug-free. I loved drugs, and if I were to only focus on the good times that I had indulging myself with them, then it would be very tempting to go back. A lot of people do this, and it is why they continually relapse. I think that initially in recovery, we need to focus wholly on ourselves and in a sense, be purposely selfish about it, but as we progress and grow, I believe that we have to take more weight for the things that happened because of us. When talking to other people after Santa Fe's death, they would say things like, "If she hadn't gotten it from you, she would have gotten it from someone else." However, the reality is that she didn't. I introduced her to drugs, and I have to bear that responsibility. Four kids have no parents, because of the life that I introduced her to. In carrying some of that weight and taking on part of that burden, I can stand stronger in my resolve never to do drugs again. However, it would be years before I would even consider taking real steps towards recovery.

Chapter 12:

Meeting My Companion

By the age of twenty-five, it was fairly typical for me to go six days at a time without sleep. Just as I did when I was dating Santa Fe, I would stay up throughout the entire week and sleep for only one day, although now that day was Sunday. I would use throughout the week, going without sleep until each Sunday when I would pop a handful of Xanax and drink several glasses of wine to knock myself out. That would be my sleep for the week. After that, I would be up and using again, going another week at a time without rest. I used to joke that if God could have a day off to rest, then so could I, and that was why Sundays were my day of rest.

Meanwhile, the shadow person that I had started seeing was morphing into something much darker and more terrifying. Most people are unable to see shadow people even within the throws of drug addiction, yet some report seeing one or even several groups of them. When I was alone, I saw just one solitary figure. However, when I was around other people using, I could see shadowy forms surrounding them too.

My Companion, as I came to know him, began as a shadowy figure that I was unable to focus on, but gradually he became more evident to me. I started hearing the grating sound of whispers that, at first, were difficult to decipher. Over time they gained clarity until I could hear him speaking directly to me. At first, the voice seemed somewhat harmless, only egging on my already existent drug use or affirming the negative thoughts that I allowed myself to voice. As if growing bolder over time, it progressed from a whisper to a scream, pressing me to do horrible things to myself and others. It shrieked in my ears, yelling and nagging me to take actions that seemed too despicable even for me.

Then one day, My Companion appeared before me. Usually hiding in the periphery, I saw something out of the corner of my eye and turned to face it. Instead of shrinking back into the shadows, it was there in front of me. A figure of darkness, he had stepped into the light, yet the light seemed to almost bend around him as if he repelled it somehow with his very being.

After that, he was always there, and unlike most shadow people who dissipate with sleep or cessation of drugs, he didn't go away. Even when I was in treatment and not using, he was there, and this scared me more than anything. I knew that this was not typical and I couldn't explain it away. Strangely enough, the presence of My Companion changed the system of beliefs that I had long clung to. A longtime atheist, my views altered to agnosticism as this ever-present supernatural evil being continued to show himself to me.

Everyone has a conscience, that inner voice that tells you right from wrong, but instead of hearing the inner guide of good, My Companion screamed hate and destruction into me. Unrelenting, he always pushed me to do darker and viler things. He always wanted me to hurt either myself or other people. Frequently he lurked in the shadows, but when I was the angriest or depressed, he would push himself to the forefront. If I were going to do something underhanded, he would prod me to do it in the worst, most rash way possible. If I were going to collect money, he would tell me to take my gun. If I were in a fight, his voice would coach me to continue kicking and punching long after the fight was over. If I were in a house with strangers that I didn't know, he would speak doubt into my ears, "They want to kill you. They are going to kill you if you don't get to them first."

If I contemplated quitting drugs, he would remind me repeatedly of all the times that I had tried to get sober and had failed. "You have been using for over half of your life. You're never going to be able to quit. This is the only thing that you are good at. You know you want to get high. You can't live without it."

As he spoke lies into my heart and thoughts, I couldn't stop seeing the terrible image of him. I stopped looking in mirrors, for the most part, because I would always see him there, lurking in the background. I also hated mirrors because they showed me the shocking image of the wicked person that I had become. My eyes would stare cold and distant, devoid of humanity, so similar to the cold dead eyes of my evil grandfather. Often when I was around the children of friends, I would hear them call my eyes "monster eyes." Eyes devoid of life and hope, they would transform from green to bright blue when I became angry. The turmoil that I had inside, evident even in my appearance.

One Sunday evening, I woke up and examining my life's pattern realized that I was never going to get sober. I was so tired of who I was and the way that I had been living but felt powerless to do anything about it. My sister had stopped by and given me a tough-love conversation. It was the drugs or her, and I chose drugs. My Companion screeched at me, his red eyes boring holes through my soul, reminding me of my worthlessness and urging me to end my life and kill myself. Over the years, I have seen several of my friends over-dose and die right in front of me, and I knew that this was where I was one day headed. I retrieved a bottle of wine, washed down some Xanax, took a nice hot bath, and slashed one of my wrists. In a voice more grating than the grinding of glass, my companion screeched at me, "Are you a coward? Don't just slash one wrist. Slash the other one too." I complied, slashing the other wrist.

Worried about the way she had left me, my sister drove by my place to check on me. Seeing my car, but not being able to get in touch with me by phone, she let herself into my apartment. She found me unconscious in a pool of blood, collapsed on the floor next to the bathtub. The bathwater was a soupy crimson red from the blood oozing out of my wrists as my life slowly leached away. Without a pulse or signs of breath, my sister thought that she had found me dead, but managed to compose herself enough to call 911. The paramedics were dispatched and managed to resuscitate me—this was the fifth time in my twenty-five years that I had died and been revived.

I was given blood transfusions and driven to the hospital. Once there, my sister begged me to make a promise to her that I would never try to kill myself again. I told her that I wouldn't, but in my heart knew that this was more or less a lie. I may not have directly tried to end my life after that, but I began to live with an increased sense of recklessness. I didn't really care if I lived or died, so I placed myself in increasingly dangerous situations. I intentionally went to houses or other environments that I knew were unsafe, and I didn't care about what could possibly happen to me. Throughout, My Companion pushed me in my reckless pursuit of destruction.

Driven by this new reckless attitude, I established an annual birthday ritual of playing Russian roulette. Yearly on the anniversary of my birth in Devil's Lake, I would tramp out alone to one of my favorite party locations in the countryside of Forsyth, Missouri. Once there, I would empty my .38 of bullets, leaving a lone bullet chambered. I would spin the revolver, gambling on the pull of the trigger. For four years, I played this deadly game, and thankfully, the gun never went off. Despite my dark companion's poisonous persistence, the hand of something far more powerful was protecting me.

Chapter 13:

Reckless

I continued to live life recklessly, risking more in the pursuit of getting high and making money. By this point, I was only actively making a few batches of meth a year. Mostly, I bought it from cooks that I knew really well locally. I also would run down to Texas, getting marijuana and meth outside of Houston and then would bring it back to Missouri to sell. I would travel down there about once a month and pick up a kilo of meth and ten pounds of marijuana. My contacts in Texas would pack it into a full-sized spare tire, which I would use to replace my own tire and then drive it back to Missouri.

At one point, I lost my connection and was given a new one by a kid that I knew. Needless to say, this was a mistake. The very first time that I returned from picking up from my new contact, I was pulled over. I was asleep in the back seat while a kid who I thought was solid drove, yet woke up to an officer with a gun pulled on me. Stopped in Texarkana, Arkansas, the cops went straight to my trunk, and I was arrested on brand new charges. In the end, they only charged me with having five pounds of marijuana, because the other five pounds and the meth somehow turned up missing.

I was put right back on probation, which I had transferred to Taney County, Missouri, where the city of Branson is located. Unfortunately, this did not slow me down.

The one positive about getting put on probation this time is that I had a probation officer who did not immediately write me off. Her name was Sallie, and she genuinely cared. This didn't stop me from using. However, it did make me take some precautions that I had previously implemented in the past to avoid getting caught. Two days before I would be scheduled to see her, I would stop using and drink a ton of fluids, praying that I would be able to pass any tests that she gave me. This had been a pattern that worked for years, so I expected it to continue working.

It was not a perfect system, though, and one time when I was scheduled to see her, I was so sick from the opioid withdrawal that I shot up right before I went to see her. I then worried that she would see me down and question the reasoning behind it, so I used meth to reverse that effect. After shooting up, I became really paranoid, so I took some Xanax to calm myself down. I can't imagine what I looked like when I went to see her, but she sat me down and asked me a simple question, "If I were to do a UA (urinalysis) on you, what would it show?"

"Honestly, I don't know what it wouldn't show," I replied.

She gave me the UA anyway, and it lit up from all the drugs in my system. It was beyond evident that I had been using. She told me that since I had been honest with her, she would give me a break. At the time, I had a ten year back up from my Arkansas charges, and I am convinced that due to my attitude and outlook, I would have ended up serving all ten years of that time. However, she had compassion for me and chose to send me to rehab instead. I only remember going to rehab once, but in fact, I was in four times in a little over a year. I do remember that when I got out, I wanted to show the world that this time, I was serious. I didn't use while I was in rehab, and I stayed sober for over a month after I got out. Two months was the longest time up to that point that I had been able to stay sober in my seventeen years of using. When I finally quit years later, those two months would still be the record for the longest time prior that I ever stayed abstinent.

A hitch developed in my plan to remain sober as a colossal bill popped up. I had worked out a deal with another drug dealer to purchase a house that they owned and during that time, I had been paying them monthly payments. They had been arrested a few months earlier, and unbeknownst to me instead of paying the mortgage, they had been giving my house payments to their lawyer to help bail them out of trouble. I was shocked to find out that I would lose my house if I didn't come up with four thousand dollars within thirty days. To raise funds fast, I drove down to Texas to pick up a couple of pounds of methamphetamine to purchase and redistribute.

Using again, I went on the worst run that I had ever gone on. I stayed up without sleep for an entire month, selling the drugs in the nearby Missouri cities of Springfield and Joplin, in addition to Branson. In the final two weeks, I had to pay someone to drive me around, because I couldn't focus enough to drive myself. Paranoia convinced me that we were being followed, so I also paid someone to write down the license plate numbers as well as the makes and models of vehicles that we came across. By the end of the month, I paid off all of the money that I owed.

After some inclement weather, I ended up stranded in the city of Springfield, Missouri, and decided to stay with some people who had been selling meth for me during this run. Unfortunately, the people that I was staying with slipped something into the last of my meth, causing me to tumble into a weeklong psychotic snap. I became convinced that there was a red laser light targeting me whenever I faced the windows and was sure that I was going to shot. Out of my mind with fear, I made everyone stay inside and refused to let anyone open the doors or windows. Paranoia and prodding from My Companion were wreaking havoc on my life.

Not long after my paranoid breakdown in Springfield, I was again in a terrible situation with My Companion right beside me, egging me on. My live-in girlfriend had turned me into the cops while I had a large amount of meth in my house. I had placed a gun to my girlfriend's head, determined to kill her for turning me in. My Companion wanted me to kill her—I wanted to kill her. Ignoring her pleas and protests to stop, I had been overwhelmed with the urge to obey My Companion and end her life. I had warred with him and had barely won, releasing my girlfriend and warning her never to return.

"You have one hour to get your stuff and go," I threatened. "You have until tomorrow to be gone for good. You are going to leave the state and go back home. I never want to see you again, or it will be a bad deal."

Whether terrorized by my threats or possibly catching sight of the demonic form looming near her, she was stunned into silence. She didn't speak—simply nodded and ran out the door. I never saw or heard from her again. She left everything behind—her clothes, make-up, purse...everything. She simply vanished.

Chapter 14:

How Bad a Substance Use Disorder Can Get

Amazingly enough, I was released from probation not long after this incident. Meanwhile, my methamphetamine and opiate usage were worse than they ever had been. In six months, I woke up in intensive care on three separate occasions—all from having overdosed. Each time I was told that I had stopped breathing and was pronounced dead. In my recklessness, I didn't even care—after each hospital release, I would be high within a week. Once, while in intensive care, I arranged to have people smuggle morphine in a syringe to me so that I could shoot up staying my withdrawal.

Back in my Desperado days, while working at Mesquite Charlie's, I used to take pains to keep other people from knowing that I shot up, hiding the marks by injecting myself in the legs or other unseen places. The physical abuse that I endured as a child made me excel at keeping secrets. Years later, I still went by the name Desperado, but I no longer cared about hiding my use. My Companion kept whispering, and I became more and more reckless with my life and behavior.

I didn't care about my life, and most of my so-called friends didn't care about me either. One weekend, on a trip to St. Louis, I rented a hotel with some friends. We had reserved the room from Friday night until Monday morning, but after the first night, I almost died. I did a shot and immediately started throwing up blood, collapsing unconscious onto the bed. My friends did nothing to help me, hanging a "Do Not Disturb" sign on the door and leaving me there soaked in my own blood and vomit. I was out cold the entire weekend. On Monday morning, when I was supposed to have been checked out, I awoke to screams of horror from the maid as she walked in to clean the room and, instead, found me unconscious in a pool of my own blood.

Soon after that incident, I was partying with a friend, and he gave me some cocaine from his private stash. My sister was living in a house by the lake, and I stopped in to spend the weekend with her. She was asleep when I arrived, so I let myself in and went straight to the bathroom to shoot up. As soon as I did it, I went blind and collapsed on the floor, the right side of my body clinching in spasms every twenty seconds. What seemed like forever was probably only a couple of minutes as I regained my eyesight. Convinced that I was going to die and not wanting my sister to find the body, I gathered up all of my drugs and paraphernalia, packing it into a bag before proceeding to jump into the lake. I hoped that I would float away so that my sister would not have to discover my body.

Once again, I somehow survived. It seemed like I had been floating in the lake for hours, but in reality, it was most likely only about thirty minutes. Once the right side of my body stopped clenching, I pulled myself out of the lake and went inside to call the friend who had given me the cocaine. I wanted to figure out what had happened and why it had such an adverse effect on my body. We talked and figured things out together. At his house, we had used the last batch that he had to sell, so when I asked for more, he had to get it out of his uncut stash. Forgetting to tell me it was stronger, upon arriving at my sister's house, I injected the same amount that I had just injected at his place, and it hit me hard.

"Are you mad at me?" He asked, warily.

"How could I be mad at you? I have never been that high before. That was awesome!"

My judgment was so skewed that I didn't care that I could have died, I just cared about the high. My Companion kept pushing me—take the drugs, jump into the lake, consume more and more…no matter what the cost.

Shortly after this incident, I had a drug deal gone wrong. One of my friends was shot in the leg, and I fired back, hitting the kid who shot him. A scar on my shoulder bears witness to the fact that this was not my first gunfight, but thankfully it was to be my last. The person that I shot lived, and this fact angered me greatly. Usually, I disagreed with My Companion as to the extent that I should push violence or harmful behavior and never went quite as far as he wanted me to go, but this time was different, and it scared me. I had reached a point where I was actually in agreement with My Companion. I was upset that I hadn't killed this guy, and I wanted him dead. The realization that I was at a point where my desires aligned with that of My Companion scared me.

Jarred by the intertwining thoughts of My Companion and myself, it dawned on me that I wanted to be done with it all. I wanted to be out of the drug game. I stopped using, but the next day the drug cravings got to be so bad that I caved and got high again. Discouraged and hearing My Companion's voice, I resigned myself to the knowledge that I would never get sober. I knew that I was going to die in my addiction, but felt helpless to do anything about it. As I wrestled with these feelings, I got the opportunity to pick up another round of drugs from Houston, Texas. Using a rental car, I retrieved it without a hitch and then set about distributing it locally in the Branson area.

In the months leading up to this, the COMET (Combined Ozarks Multi-Jurisdictional Enforcement Team) had identified me as a source for drugs and had been specifically targeting me. They had raided my house twice, had hit my friend's house while I was there, and I had two other close encounters with them. For a long time, they had linked the name Desperado with drug distribution in the area and other illegal acts, but now they finally connected that name with mine—David Stoecker was on their radar. They definitely knew who I was, and I was terrified that they were closing in on me.

This fear was magnified when I had another severe psychotic break. Either from the meth that I had just brought back or possibly from dope, I had a worse break than the time that I locked myself in the home in Springfield.

Convinced that the task force was going to get me finally, I barricaded the doors and windows on the ground floor of my sister's house, not allowing anyone in or out. My sister had to call-in to miss work for several days as I refused to let her leave the house. My Companion's voice was shrieking in my ear, growing louder and louder while I paced around the house with a loaded gun keeping the imagined police officers at bay and ordering their helicopters to stay in the air. Only none of it was actually occurring—there were no police officers there and no helicopters. Sure, I was firmly on the police force's radar, but they were not at the house. Eventually, I let my sister out, and when she later returned home, the house was torn apart. I explained that I had gotten into a fight with several people while she was gone.

"I can't believe that you sent an intervention team in here to send me away," I chastised her.

Confused, but recognizing what had occurred, she replied. "I didn't send anyone here. It has been you here by yourself the whole time."

Confident that she was wrong, I instructed her to follow me around the house, eager to show her what had happened. I went into the bathroom to show her the blood pooling from where I had smashed one of the guys with the back of the toilet, but there was no blood and no body—only broken porcelain. I had imagined the whole thing and had been fighting with myself. I felt like I was losing my mind. My sister and I had a discussion, and we agreed that something had to change.

I took a couple of Xanax so that I could come down from my high and allow myself to think more clearly. After that, I slept for a day and a half. When I woke up, I packed a duffle bag full of clothes and rented a car. I told my friends that I was going to Houston, yet in reality, I was not even leaving the state. I drove down the highway for less than an hour and ended up in Springfield, Missouri. I left behind my house and my cars—I wanted to leave my past behind me and knew that if I were still paying for those things, then I would eventually resort to selling drugs to pay for it. To stop the carousel of mayhem and leave everything in the past, I would give up everything, even if that meant the bank taking back all of my possessions. To keep my belongings at the expense of doing something illegal to pay for them meant they were no longer worth the cost. I wanted a new start in a new town. I was done!

Chapter 15:

Unrelenting Evil

I desperately needed to escape. Just as My Companion had grown more prominent over time, so had the despair that I felt as I descended further and further into the mire of drugs and violence. I loved drugs and the feeling that they gave me, but the cost had become too high.

My Companion was always speaking evil into me—evil thoughts, evil deeds. I knew that if something didn't change, I would end up killing either myself or someone else.

When my shadow person appeared before me, coming out of the shadows and began speaking directly to me, I started to believe in the supernatural. I knew that My Companion was evil and that he was a spirit or demonic presence of some sort, so if he existed, then other spirits must exist as well.

My Companion was unrelenting in his desire to drown me in destruction. It wasn't just me that he was trying to destroy. He was using me to wreck the lives of others as well. I was distributing drugs and profiting from addiction, while people all around me were disappearing, starving, living in homelessness, overdosing, and dying. I lived a life of violence, even though I had seen a good friend beaten to death right in front of me. I drove drunk and high and put other people's lives in danger. I almost murdered my girlfriend. I shot and tried to kill a rival. I stole a car to ditch a friend at the hospital after he blew himself up in a meth lab explosion. Friend after friend was convicted and sentenced to anywhere from ten to twenty-five years in prison. I had recruited others to join my army of evil, drowning everything, and everyone in our destructive wake.

Car accidents, Russian roulette, suicide attempts, over-amping (overdosing on methamphetamine), dying eight times on six different occasions, car accidents, fights, concussions, prison time—I had drawn so many lines in the sand as to what I would and wouldn't do, only to stomp all over them. My Companion was always pushing me, but I was also a champion at justifying all of my behavior. I justified my yearly Russian roulette by saying that if it killed me, it wasn't due to my own actions, but the fickle hand of fate or chance intervening. For the longest time, I never touched heroin, because, in my mind, that was something that only junkies did. The funny thing was that I had a friend who did heroin who would never touch meth for that exact same reason. The truth was that no amount of justifying could ever rationalize or wipe away my actions.

In my years spent serving My Companion, I had come to feel more relaxed in jail than on the street. In part, because I had spent a lot of time in jail—approximately twenty stays in about twelve years. When I was in jail, no one was trying to rob me, shoot me, raid my house, or bust me, and that actually gave me a sense of relief. Sometimes, even when I had enough money to bond myself out already in my wallet, I would sit there for a couple of weeks, finding an almost calm in the turbulence of my life. Usually, while in jail, I would stay off meth but have pills snuck in to me so I wouldn't go into detox while I slept and ate for a few weeks. Once I had rested and regained some healthy weight, I would bond out. If it were too stressful in the main population, then I would start a fight to move into maximum security. Even when off of meth, My Companion was still there.

That was my life back then—drugs, jail, fighting, bartending, waiting tables, overdosing, going without sleep, seeing friends die, and watching people destroy their lives. My Companion was constant in his use of me to create a path of carnage and destruction everywhere I went. Everyone that I met, I brought down or made worse. Even with My Companion always there, I felt utterly alone. I didn't have real friends. I just had people that I used. If they couldn't help me, then I had no use for them, and I became tired of living like this. I didn't make friends, I took hostages. I might have had a couple of friends who would have taken bullets for me, but for the right amount of money, they would have equally gladly put a bullet in me.

I was tired of my life the way it was, tired of being surrounded by people who had no care or concern for the future. I may have been told that I was a lost cause and beyond repair, but I was ready to show people that I could be different. I was ready for a sober life… or so I thought.

Chapter 16:

Alcohol is a Drug

I showed up at my mom's house with nothing but a duffel bag full of clothes. Not sure what to do or where to turn, I ended up on her doorstep. She was not exactly pleased to see me, as, by this point, I had stolen from her so many times that she did not trust me in her house alone. Her lack of trust was something that I had definitely earned and was justified.

"What are you doing here?" She questioned as she opened the door.

"I have three choices, Mom. I can either continue living my life the way I am and one of these times when I die--I won't come back. They won't be able to save me." She knew that this statement bore validity.

"I can get arrested again, which I will never let happen. I will make them kill me before I'll go back to prison," I said. "Or, you can let me stay here until I get back on my feet. I am ready to quit using."

Amazingly, she opened the door and let me it. I stayed there for about six months. For the first few days, I did nothing but sleep.

Rested and off of drugs, another amazing thing happened. My Companion disappeared and never returned. For over six years, he had been with me everywhere, and now he was gone. At the time, I was uncertain what to think, but after years of education and training, including my work talking with thousands of people in a clinical setting, I believe there are two ways that you can view this phenomenon. It can either be viewed as a constant psychotic episode, which is certainly possible. However, up until this point, My Companion had never disappeared. Not even with rest, or the few months that I had been in treatment or managed to stay previously sober. Alternately, it can be seen through the lens that I tend to view it with, which is that the use of intravenous drugs opened or weakened the barrier between the spiritual and physical realm, inviting evil through an open door into my life. Whether you believe as I do that it was a demonic presence, or that it was just a psychotic break, the fact is that when I stood up to it, making the decision to end my drug use, it disappeared completely.

While staying with my mom, I met up with a residential tech who agreed to be my sponsor. I started attending twelve-step recovery meetings and working through the twelve steps with him. My sponsor, Jay, wanted me to attend ninety meetings in ninety days. Just as I passionately pursued drugs before this, I dove full force into recovery, attending 150 meetings in ninety days. After meetings, I went out to coffee with others for accountability every chance that I got. I was serious about not using drugs.

Meanwhile, I got a job in a restaurant, and I started drinking a lot. I still considered myself sober as I was no longer doing drugs, but what I didn't acknowledge is that alcohol is, in actuality, a drug. It may be a socially acceptable drug, but it is still a drug. In fact, it is a drug that kills more people than all of the other drugs (other than nicotine) combined. I applied my excess for more as equally to drinking as I did to staying off of drugs. Initially, I confined my drinking to the weekends, getting drunk only once a week, but after moving out of my mom's house, my alcohol use started snowballing. I would go out with my coworkers during the week as well as on the weekends, getting drunk every time I went out.

During this time, I was still moving forward with trying to establish a life and a future for myself. I discovered that the score from the General Education Diploma (GED) test that I had taken while in prison several years before, was actually high enough that it qualified me to receive a scholarship for college. Excited about this prospect, I went to Vocational Rehab, where they sent me to get a neuropsychological test given to me throughout two days. When the testing was complete, the assessor explained to me that my short-term memory was shot due to the multiple concussions and head traumas that I had sustained over the years, and this was additionally made worse by my prolonged drug use. He encouraged me by saying that I was intelligent, and there was a possibility that my memory could come back; however, he also cautioned me that it could never return.

Undeterred, I began attending classes at the local community college, Ozark's Technical College (OTC), in the fall of 2002. Most of my first year of college was a constant struggle, but I tried to implement the strategies that my assessor had given me to succeed. My assessment qualified me to be able to have additional time to take tests, but I still had to read and reread—being diligent to write things down on index cards to continually review them. I used repetition techniques to try to get things locked into my long-term memory instead of lost in my unreliable short-term memory.

Over that first year, my memory started to come back, and by the end of the year, I was getting straight A's. I also made new friends to party with. Drinking became a way of life for me. Perhaps a reflection of the functioning alcoholic my dad had been when I was little, I now would drink almost every other night during the week and throughout the weekend. I was still managing well in school, though, and by 2003 I was going to school at OTC full time in earnest pursuit of a degree.

I graduated with honors from OTC and was able to receive a transfer scholarship to Southwest Missouri State University (SMSU). Located in the center of Springfield, SMSU would later change its name to Missouri State University (MSU).

By this time, I was drinking just about every night—usually to the point of blacking out. Obviously, not learning much from all my car accidents and drunk driving incidents of the past, I am ashamed to say that I would still drive every time that I went out to drink. I would wake up with no memory of my drive home the previous night and somehow find this to be funny. I justified my behavior just as I always had done in the past because alcohol was legal and socially acceptable.

In the midst of this, I decided that I wanted to put some weight on, and I wanted to do it quickly, so I started to do steroids, using those for approximately a year and a half. In that time, I managed to put on about one hundred pounds—a far cry from my gaunt appearance on meth. The upside of this was that I got huge, fast. My arms measured twenty inches, and I gained the ability to bench press almost five hundred pounds. The downside was that this change was too rapid, and my body was unable to balance it. I tore a tendon in my right arm that still bothers me to this day. This also caused severe damage to my lower back that has hindered my ability to play with my kids as they have gotten older.

Otherwise, things were going reasonably well, and I felt that for the first time in a long time, things were going to be ok. I began dating a girl that I really liked who was going to school to become a physical therapist. After graduate school, she planned on getting a job and in turn, helping me to get my Ph.D. in psychology. At that time, I was already working on a double major degree in psychology and sociology.

My girlfriend's dad was a police officer, and one day he called me, "You need to turn yourself in. You have a warrant out for your arrest," he said.

The raid at my house where I had been held for twenty-four hours and released was coming back to haunt me. I called my best friend for guidance, scared because I really didn't know what I was going to do. I knew that I would have to try to bond out, but I wouldn't be able to make bond. My friend said that he would be right over. When he arrived, we discussed my options, which were not good.

"I can go on the run, I can flee the country, or I can go down and turn myself in," I said resignedly. "If it is for the charge that I think it is, then I am facing at least ten years."

"Let's go to Forsyth," he suggested. "We can talk to a bondsman and have him meet us there. I got you," he reassured.

Bolstered by his support, we drove south to Forsyth, Missouri, and talked with the bondsman. He made a couple of calls, and then we walked over together to turn me in. My friend paid my bond of $5,000 with the agreement that I would pay him back with my next round of student loans. I contacted an attorney who wanted one thousand dollars down as an initial retainer. I went into the police station, spent a couple of hours in booking, and then was released. Over the next few months, I would spend an additional four thousand dollars on attorney fees, appearing in court twice before the charges were dropped.

Fortunately for me, the fact that it had been over five years since the raid played in my favor. Additionally, my girlfriend had let the police into the house and given them consent to search even though I was home at the time, and the house was in my name. These facts, combined with the evidence that I was doing really well pursuing my education and not getting into trouble, all worked in my favor.

I had indeed been doing well, but this brush with potential prison time threw me into an even greater indulgence for alcohol. I had been working at the restaurant, Ruby Tuesdays, and this further enabled my drinking as there was never a night that a coworker didn't want to go drink. I began drinking more and more.

During this time, I also dealt with the harsh effects of the years of drugs I had done. I developed severe dental problems, sometimes having to miss work due to the pain from multiple cavities. I sought help through Vocational Rehab, and they agreed to pay for my dental work. I ended up having to get all of my teeth pulled, and a full set of dentures put in—just one more effect of the years of drugs and partying.

My girlfriend and I had been together for a long time, but I started cheating on her. Eventually, after almost four years together, I broke up with her. I ended things with one of the most truthful reasons I had ever given:

"We should have broken up two years ago because two years ago we stopped being happy and trying to make our partner happy. We are together because we are comfortable, and we deserve more than that. We deserve to be happy with someone who loves us. I am sorry that I wasted the last two years of your life." I was happy to be single again, but she was upset. I believe that she still hates me to this day.

That relationship over, I continued to drink and go to parties nightly. If I was out drinking, and there wasn't an after-party planned, I would have everyone back over to my house, hosting the drinking there. I was drinking to the point of blacking out every single night. If on the rare occasion I didn't drink, then I would get the shakes and not be able to sleep. There were nights that I would wake up with the shakes and have to drink a few shots of whatever was available to allow myself to fall back asleep. There were also times when I would awaken to find that I had drenched myself in urine while I slept—too out of it to notice until the morning. Alcohol may have been a more socially accepted drug of choice, but if I thought that I had found sobriety, then I was fooling myself.

I continued drinking, getting into fights, and sleeping with random women. In addition to this, I was spending three to five nights a week playing softball. There was usually always alcohol and women around the softball complex. After not dating exclusively for a while, I met a girl at the softball fields, and we hit it off and began dating.

Shortly after that, two significant events occurred. The first was that I got accepted into graduate school for a Master's degree in social work. I was about to finish my undergraduate studies, graduating with a double Bachelor's degree an overall grade point average (GPA) of 3.7. Proud of what I had accomplished, I set my sights on social work as I thought it would benefit me more than a Psychology graduate degree. The second occurrence was by far the more important—my girlfriend got pregnant.

I wish that I could say that the fact that I was going to be a dad pushed me to alter my drinking behavior, but it didn't. My drinking didn't slow down at all. My son was born prematurely, and at 33.5 weeks along, his tiny lungs struggled to support his body. Even while he fought for life in the NICU, I was still drinking daily. Sometimes I drank just to avoid the shakes, but usually, I drank a lot more than that. I justified my drinking as I had justified everything else. I had become a functional alcoholic just like my own father had been, but because I was still moving forward, I justified it all. I was still working full-time, playing softball at least three nights a week, and maintaining A's and B's in school. My life was full, yet I was miserable, feeling vacant inside.

I was only happy when I was drunk, and that is only because then I was too drunk to evaluate just how poorly my life was really going. I had no purpose...no real direction. I had reached extreme heights in my ability to justify my actions as I was now a full-blown alcoholic who was working in a treatment center as part of my University's practicum program. I was working with other people who struggled with addictions while I was submerged in my own. Since alcohol was not illegal, I justified this to myself. After all, in comparison, I was no longer using the needle. Addicts are truly master manipulators and validators, not just to others, but to ourselves as well.

Generations of us have sworn that we would never be like our parents, only to become replicas of precisely what we are trying to avoid, and I was no different. I hated my father's alcoholism and the duality and hypocrisy of the lives that my parents lived, yet here I was doing the same thing now that I was a dad myself. I had my own son, was pursuing my Master's degree, and yet I was out getting drunk every night. On the rare nights that I wouldn't drink, I would instead drink throughout the day to avoid the shakes. I was working in a position where I pretended to be ok, much like my parents used to pretend that they were the perfect Jehovah's Witnesses. I would have loved to inherit some of the positive characteristics that my parents had, but it seemed that I only inherited their negative traits. I had become the very embodiment of the hypocrisy I hated so much in them.

Chapter 17:

Defeated but Not Destroyed

Well after midnight, I awoke to county sheriff knocking at my door. Before he uttered a single word, I knew why he was there, and it shook me to my core. My dad was dead.

My dad had stayed with me the previous year. Desiring to be around for the birth of my son, he had moved in before the due date. Unfortunately, due to his bipolar disorder, he was in the clutches of a full-blown manic episode. The medication that he was on had not been helping. As a result of this, he was causing a lot of stress to my son's mother. After several serious conversations with him, that didn't alter his behavior in the least, I told him that he was no longer welcome in my house. That was the last time I would ever see him.

He left in May of 2007, doing a farewell tour of sorts. In retrospect, he was spending time with family each member and everyone that he was close to, burning bridges with each one to justify his final actions. After leaving my house, he visited my sister doing his best to make her as mad as possible. Then, he spent a week with his brother, where he was asked to leave as well. As he traveled across the country, he was also rapidly burning through thousands of dollars, blowing through his retirement and maxing out all of his credit cards. My stepmom, Linda, who loved him enough to put up with his unpredictable behavior for years, had to file for divorce to protect her credit from his continued financial destruction. I now understand that my dad was doing his best to enrage everyone, isolating himself, and spending the last of his resources. This way, when he started to crash in his depressed phase, he would be able to tell himself that he had nothing, and no one was in his corner. He was providing himself excuses for his justifications of his own.

After alienating everyone that he was close to, my dad headed back to where he had been living in Florida. On February 11th, I received a call from my dad. He sounded really down—lower than I had ever heard him before. I tried to offer him some helpful suggestions to keep him busy and elevate his mood level. I also reminded him that in May, I would be coming to Florida to visit him and that he would finally get to meet his grandson. Usually discussing this would help lift his mood, but instead, all he could focus on was how much everyone hated him, the Dodgers leaving Florida for spring training in Arizona, and all the money that he owed. Nothing that I said cheered him up.

The last words that I said to him were, "I love you, and I can't wait to see you this summer." I also told him that I was trying to be half the dad to my son that he was to me. I really loved my dad.

After I got off the phone with him, I immediately initiated a conference call with my sister and my stepmom to discuss my concerns about my father with them. We were all apprehensive but decided that due to my dad's faith and the fact that he had just been released from the hospital for stabilization to his mental health less than a week previous, that he would not commit suicide.

On February 12, 2008, when I opened the door, coming face to face with the sheriff, I knew that my dad was gone.

"It's about your dad," he said.

"Do you know how he killed himself?" I responded instinctually.

He didn't know but directed me to call a detective in Florida who was trying to get in touch with me. I remember closing the door and breaking down laughing—I was in shock. My laughter was an intense reaction to the pain. My dad was my hero, my superman. I couldn't believe that he was gone.

My brain was racing by the time I got off the phone with the detective in Florida. I had not talked to my dad as much as I should have, because I always figured that there would be more time to do it after I had graduated from college. Now, my son would never get to meet him. My dad would never get to see me sober. I would never be able to talk to my dad again …ever. This hurt so much.

At first, I took his suicide personally, making it all about me. How could he do this to me? I was flooded with self-pity—*poor me, feel sorry for me, have pity on me. Me. Me. Me.* My thoughts were utterly self-centered. I didn't take the time to consider what my sister was going through, my stepmother's grief, or how my baby brother was processing the trauma of finding his dad's body. All I thought about was how it impacted me and what a selfish choice my dad had made. Eventually, I began to imagine what he had been going through and realized that he was miserable and unable to see a way out. He was in pain…a more profound sadness than I had realized. He did not want to hurt anymore, and in death, he could relax, be free. For him, it was all about him…feeling like the world would be better without him in it.

Just as I was wrong in my own selfish thinking, he was wrong, as well. The world was not better off without him, and suicide is truly not a victimless crime. Suicide leaves people behind, ever wondering if they are to blame or if they could have said or done something that might have changed the outcome. My dad was dead; his battle was waged and over with. The dead are gone. They have moved on. It is the survivors that are left struggling to find out how to move forward, how to live life without the person we loved that left us so suddenly. Waves of grief wash over us, and we have to find a way to live in our new normal. I didn't know how to do that. How would I move on or function in a world without my dad? I did not know how to cope other than using drugs to escape. At first, I wanted to do a big shot of dope, but thankfully a friend talked me out of it. Instead, I drank as I had never drunk before. I tried to drown in alcohol to numb myself from the overwhelming feelings of loss.

After my dad's death, I traveled to Florida to attempt to find some answers as well as escape from the truth. I drank while I tried to make sense of what had happened. I drank a lot, but no matter how much I drank, I could not escape from the truth. I could not hide from it even for one minute. I tried to hide it like I had my past traumas, compartmentalizing it and stashing it behind walls that I had built up over the years, then running away from it with intoxication. This time was different, though. No matter how I tried not to think about it, I still did. I could not run away or numb my feelings. All I felt was hopeless and empty.

In the past, I was able to numb myself with drugs or use sex or violence to flood my neurotransmitters with massive amounts of good feeling chemicals in my brain, to destroy my anguish. This time was different. It didn't matter how many people I slept with, how much I drank, or how much I physically hurt myself or others…the pain would not go away. I couldn't avoid the tortured feelings inside of me. I could not get over what had happened. I had always been able to resurface after my own defeats, but now I was crushed and felt forever broken.

My father made a decision. He devised a permanent solution to a temporary problem. He did what he felt was right and left the rest of us behind in shock and pain. He was my superman, my role model, my hero…now he was gone. The last time that I had seen him in person, I had said things that I would never be able to take back or apologize for in a face to face conversation. When he died, I felt like I had been stripped of the ability to make amends, and that felt terrible. I grappled with feelings of shame and anguish.

My life was forever changed, but I forgave him. His death was the result of his bipolar disorder, not being appropriately treated. Afterward, I remember viewing the security footage of him shopping at the drugstore for some of the supplies that he would later use to take his own life. He had a big smile on his face while he shopped, knowing that his fight would soon be over. For years he had yo-yoed, going from manic highs to devastating lows before bouncing back up again. He had a pattern of being admitted to an institution for treatment and undergoing stabilization through medication, only to stop the meds six months or a year later due to missing the way he felt and the energy he had when he was in the highs of a manic episode. I get it…I am bipolar as well. I forgave him.

Forgiving myself would be far more difficult. I hated myself and wallowed in self-loathing. I should have known better. I was the last person to talk to him, and I saw the warning signs. If he had been a client who I was working with during my practicum, I would have had him held on a psych hold. He wasn't someone that I worked with though…he was my dad. I had heard it before—the sadness and hopelessness, but I second-guessed myself. It would be a long time before I got over that.

I was ill-prepared to face the situation, especially as it wasn't anything that I wanted to address, to begin with. So, I stayed drunk in Florida. I cannot begin to imagine how hurtful my actions were to my stepmom and baby brother, who was only twelve at the time. I drank and drank and drank some more. When I finally did return to Springfield and life in Missouri, I drank more and lashed out more, taking out my anguish and anger on everyone around me.

It wasn't long before I broke up with my son's mom. She took my son and at first wouldn't let me see him at all. Gradually, she allowed me to see him for an hour a month, stationing her family all around the park where we met, in case I was going to run off or kidnap my son. Honestly, it was a good thing that her family was there, standing guard, or I probably would be in prison or still on the run for kidnapping my son. Neither prison or going on the run would have been beneficial for my son or me. Luckily, I avoided making that poor decision.

The week following my break up with my girlfriend, I found out that the place I had completed my practicum at had hired me to work as a Community Support Specialist (CSS). I was now employed at a residential and outpatient treatment center, yet I was also drinking to blackout every single night. I could not consume enough alcohol. There was also not enough alcohol to drown my pain this time. There was nowhere to hide, and I was lower than I had ever been. I was working as a CSS full-time, going to college full-time, working weekends at Ruby Tuesdays, and yet I was still drinking as if it were my sole career.

Chapter 18:

My Recovery

For years, I had worked with a really great guy at Ruby Tuesdays named Nate. His wife, Becca, was really wonderful too. I got to know Becca during her visits to Nate while he was working his shifts. She also would fill in with my softball team from time to time. I got along with both of them pretty well...considering they were Christians. An angry, nonbeliever for the majority of my life, I often used my disbelief in God, coupled with my intelligence, to make fun of Christians. I generally thought that most Christians' faith in God was annoying and needed to be crushed, so I took advantage of every opportunity to do this. Most of my past experiences with Christians were terrible, and I understood them to be judgmental hypocrites and hate mongers.

Nate and Becca were different, though. They truly cared about people. Their compassion was genuine, so they earned my respect. They would sometimes ask me if they could pray for me. My reply was always the same, "It can't hurt. Knock yourself out."

As I was processing my dad's death, not being able to see my son, and living the complicated lie of a double life at the treatment center, Nate reached out to me.

"I have never seen you this depressed, David. I know you have a lot of stuff going on in your life right now, and I think that you need to be around some people who care about you. Becca and I would love for you to come with us to church this Sunday."

I laughed at Nate and told him that I was not stepping foot in church unless it was for a funeral or wedding.

"You were lucky to get me into a church for your wedding, Nate. I can't stand church, and I can't stand Christians," I stated emphatically.

A couple of weeks later, he invited me again. Again, I laughed and told him, "No." A few weeks went by, and one day Becca stopped into Ruby Tuesdays to eat lunch with Nate while he was on his break. I said hi to her. She smiled at me.

"David, I hate seeing you so sad," she gently prodded. "I saw you were off this Sunday, and I would love for you to join us. We are going to BBQ and listen to live music."

I looked at her and said, "I love BBQ and music. I'll come hang out with you guys."

She winked at me and said, "Awesome, it starts right after church gets over."

That Sunday, I met Nate and Becca at their church. I sat with them during the service, and we talked during the barbecue and music. They introduced me to Becca's mom Julie, and she plied me with questions, and I would give her my answers. She was tenacious, and for every question that I answered, it felt like she would ask two more.

After talking with Becca's mom, another lady came over and introduced herself to me. She was a counselor who told me that every Sunday during the first service, they offered a recovery support group based on the ministry of Celebrate Recovery, a faith-based twelve-step program.

Next, a guy named Mike introduced himself to me. He was from Chicago and a big fan of Chicago sports teams like I was. As we talked, I found out that he went to the Sunday morning recovery support group. I told him that the next Sunday that I was off, I would give it a try.

Two weeks later, on a Sunday morning, I tried out the support group during the early service and then sat next to Nate and Becca during the second-morning church service. I decided that I liked the support group. I was not worried about seeing any of the clients that I worked with in the group, and I could be honest and open about my drinking. After the meetings, I could sit for a while with a couple of people who really cared about me, then eat lunch together following the service. After lunch together, we would part company—Nate and Becca heading off to do whatever they did after church on Sundays and me going to the bar.

Depending on my schedule, I started to go to church once or twice a month. I followed this pattern for several months. Then one night, I had a wake-up call. I began my evening at a sports bar watching a pay per view Ultimate Fighting Championship (UFC), then decided that I wanted to sing a song at a karaoke bar before the night ended, so I left and headed there when the main event ended. I made it to the karaoke bar in time to sing a song and then close down the bar. Intoxicated from an evening of drinking, I pulled out of the bar parking lot only to have a cop immediately zip in behind me.

Seeing the cop car scared me and I realized that if I got charged with "Driving While Intoxicated (DWI)," then I would go to jail. Going to jail would cause me to get kicked out of my practicum, where I was now getting paid in my second practicum, to work as a counselor. Getting kicked out of my practicum would result in me getting kicked out of graduate school. Getting kicked out of graduate school would ensure that the past six years of college would mean absolutely nothing. Unsure of what else to do, I immediately began to pray.

"God, if I don't get pulled over, I will go to church every Sunday," I bargained, checking behind me and still seeing the police car on my tail. I continued to pray.

"I promise, if I don't get pulled over, I will go to church every Sunday and will never drink again." The cop was still behind me, matching every turn. Every time I turned, and he followed me, I added another bargaining chip onto my prayer. By the time that I had made it to my street, I had promised to go to church every Sunday, quit drinking, quit smoking cigarettes, quit cussing, quit fighting, and quit having premarital sex. When I made the final turn onto my street, the police car drove straight ahead instead of turning with me.

I pulled into the garage, closed it, and passed out in my car. Passing out in my car was not unheard of for me, but the next morning was different. Usually, I would awaken with few memories of the previous night, but this time I had not blacked out. I remembered my prayers, pleas, and bartering with God. I also remembered that I had made a deal with Him. He had come through on his end of the bargain. Would I still stick to mine?

That deal withstanding, I also knew that I had plans that day to go to a Super Bowl party at my friend Josh's house. There would definitely be a lot of people smoking and drinking there. The voice that I attributed to my addiction, who I now realize was the devil, spoke to me, his doubts reverberating in my head.

Words of *you have been using drugs and drinking for over twenty years*, and *you've been smoking for over a quarter of a century...you will never quit*, played in my head like a broken record. *Go, have fun. Why try and fail again? You have tried so many times to stop before. You will never quit.*

Listening to this voice, I headed inside to take a shower to clean up and get ready for the party. I hopped in the car to head over to Josh's house, giving up before I had ever really started. Listening to the radio, I flipped the channel when a song that I didn't like came up. There was a small silence, and I waited to see what song this next station was going to play. A song by Brandon Heath played, and the very first words that I heard were, *I wish you could see me now. I wish I could show you how I'm not who I was.*

In an instant, everything changed…the voice in my head was no longer one of a tormentor. It was replaced by a much stronger voice, declaring, "You are not who you were yesterday. You can do this. You are mine."

I pulled over to the side of the road and lost it completely. I cried until the tears blinded me. I immediately knew that I was done—not just with the alcohol and drugs, but with cigarettes, cursing, fighting, and premarital sex. Everything was different. I no longer was who I had been. I now belonged to God.

As recovery is a program of progress and not perfection, I can honestly say that I have cursed a few times since then but have been drug, alcohol, premarital sex, and cigarette free. The only fight I have been in since was in a boxing ring for a PAL (Police Athletic League) Charity Fundraiser.

If I said that moment removed my craving for drugs and alcohol, that would be a lie. Life is not all cupcakes and cotton candy, so the desire to sin is still there, but the obsession is gone. Even when the desire hits, I don't pick up because when Christ came into my life, I was reborn—a new creation in Him and no longer bound to darkness.

Choosing to follow the Lord did not remove hardship. People I care about die unexpectedly—most often from overdoses, and this is hard and painful. People still lie and lash out at me, and this is hurtful. I still struggle to pay my bills sometimes, and my kids don't always listen to me, but this is the imperfect life we live in. I still wrestle with making wise decisions. Life is not easy or perfect, but I am forever changed. I don't always do the right thing, but I try. I make amends more quickly and am still trying to self-evaluate and improve. I have found that I need to apply myself to my recovery as fully as I did my addiction. I was not just addicted to one thing that I used a couple of days a week. I was addicted to multiple things that I used daily. My recovery is fueled by working on it absolutely every day. I implement various pathways to recovery; some of them are daily, weekly, or monthly, but I am always consistently moving forward. If I miss something, I don't quit. I just make sure that I do it the next time. I am still growing. I'm not who I was.

I have come to a place where I hold on to a few things about this time in my life so that I can function today:

1. I know that evil exists, and at one period in my life, I made very evil choices.

2. I know that nothing good lived in me during my addiction and that all people are capable of doing things in their lives while struggling, that they could usually never comprehend.

3. I know I am no longer the person I was when I was actively using substances, for I have found a better life in recovery

4. I know that I have made my life a living amends so that I can help rebuild other people's lives today instead of destroying them like I once did.

5. I know I believe there are multiple pathways to recovery. My path is due to my belief in a Higher Power I call Jesus Christ, which has freed me from my addiction. He supports, encourages, and guides me in all that I do today.

I wish you could see me now. I wish I could show you how I'm not who I was.

Chapter 19:

I'm Not Who I Was.

On January 31st of 2009, when I got sober, my life radically changed. I poured all the focus and energy I had for my addictions into my faith and my recovery. So much of my life has been different since that day.

I was transformed, but it didn't mean that I had all the answers or was without some doubt. I now knew that God was real, but I still had so many questions. My entire life, even in my addictions, I had maintained a voracious thirst for knowledge. An avid reader since my childhood days, I now focused on reading material that would help me find answers to the questions about faith that I still grappled with. I frequently met with my pastor to talk, study, and learn. He helped guide and direct me through those initial questions and spiritual concepts that I grappled with understanding. I also read the following books, which I recommend to others.

- The Case for Christ by Lee Strobel
- The Case for Faith by Lee Strobel

- Mere Christianity by C.S. Lewis

- What's So Amazing About Grace by Philip Yancey

- Where is God When It Hurts by Philip Yancey

- Holman QuickSource Guide to Christian Apologetics by Doug Powell

Those books helped to answer many of my questions and grow in my faith. Additionally, I studied the Bible, which continues to be the book that I use to help shape my faith and grow in wisdom and knowledge. I call it my Big Book.

I know that for some of my readers, just the mention of God might turn you away or keep you from reading further. Here's the thing, I firmly believe that there are multiple paths to recovery--many not faith-related. I share about these, so there is no need to put the book down yet. However, there was a reason that my life changed dramatically and immediately upon my salvation. Back then, I would have told you that nobody hated me more than I hated myself, and I despised myself. My inner monologue was always one that told me how I would never be good enough, that I was no good, a failure, etc. When I chose to follow Jesus, I received the Holy Spirit in my life. This was life-changing! I used to wish that I had been alive to walk with Christ here on earth, but I would argue that when Jesus ascended back into Heaven and left the Holy Spirit in his stead, we were gifted with transforming power. The Holy Spirit doesn't just walk beside us, it lives inside us, permeating our body and guiding all that we do. The Holy Spirit can give us the power to do all that God has planned for our lives. With this transformation, the Holy Spirit became my inner guide, speaking life, and hope into me instead of lies and discouragement. He has grand plans for my good, and this provides me great peace as well as inspiration.

As a practical example of what the Holy Spirit can do for you, I use this example. I am from Illinois and a huge Chicago Bulls fan. I am also a Michael Jordan fan. I believe that he can be called the greatest basketball player of all time, and most people would agree that would be a legitimate claim.

Now imagine Jordan as your coach. He is teaching you how to play better, and during the games, he tells you what plays to run. You would be a better basketball player. You would be better, but still, be limited by your own ball skills. Now, imagine that Jordan could take over your body and help control what you did. You have his skill set, his knowledge, and his vision working through you and guiding your play. Which way do you feel that you would be the best player? Would it be better for him to teach/coach you or for him to play through you? I am sure we agree that Michael Jordan playing through you would make you a better player. Jesus would have agreed with the analogy. He even told us of the greatness of the Holy Spirit.

Listen to how highly Jesus speaks of the Holy Spirit. In John 16:7-8, Jesus says, In John 16:7-8, He says, "But I tell you the truth: **It is for your good that I am going away.** Unless I go away, the Comforter will not come to you; but if I go, I will send him to you. When he comes, he will convict the world of guilt in regard to sin and righteousness and judgment.

I would say that there are absolutely no excuses that we truly can make when it comes to sin for one reason. Jesus took our ability to make excuses away from us. In John 14:26 (NIV) He says, "But the Advocate, the Holy Spirit, whom the Father will send in my name, will teach you all things and will remind you of **everything** I have said to you."

We are not only taught by the words of Christ and his disciples. We also have the Holy Spirit inside of us to remind us of what is right, like a moral compass. We will know right from wrong, and we will know our sin is a sin before we do it. Christ does not give us a way out. Will we all still sin? Of course, we will, sadly, it is in our nature. But we must learn from our indiscretions so that we do not continue to do them. We must learn to not rely on ourselves because we tend to make poor decisions if left on our own.

We must learn to rely on something greater than ourselves. We must rely on the Holy Spirit in our lives. We must learn to listen for His whispers in all that we do. If we can begin meditating, that is a great start. Take solace in silence and prayer. That way, we have a much better chance of hearing how the Holy Spirit would direct our lives.

But do not discount that whisper as many do. Listen, and then take action. Sin is not a good thing; it is not as minor an issue as many people think that it is. We will have to give account for our lives one day. Based on that and the words in the Bible, sin is a major issue and needs to be overcome at all costs. We need to nourish ourselves spiritually on a daily basis.

Yet we will still attempt to make excuses for our sinful nature. I know that I did that for a long time, yet Jesus would tell us that we should know right from wrong and are constantly reminded of what we should be doing. The Holy Spirit convicts us to do as God has asked us, as He has commanded us to do.

The Holy Spirit actually convicts us of right and wrong. To be convicted means to have a firmly held belief or opinion. That is what the Holy Spirit provides us with. The Holy Spirit allows us to live our lives well. We can overcome sin if we rely on the Holy Spirit that is in us.

The disciple claiming to love Jesus the most denied that he was his disciple when confronted three times in Mark 14:66-72. He loved Christ, but yet could not stand up for the person that he loved out of fear. In fact, Mark 14:50 (NIV) says, "Then everyone deserted Him and fled." These are the same disciples that all agreed with Peter, in Mark 14:31, stating that they would never disown or desert Jesus. This is how the disciples behaved before the Holy Spirit was here.

Jesus told the disciples that He had to leave so that the Holy Spirit could come. He discusses this in John 14:16, 17 (ESV), "And I will ask the Father, and he will give you another advocate to help you and be with you forever— the Spirit of truth. The world cannot accept him because it neither sees him nor knows him. But you know him, for he lives with you and will be **in you**."

After Jesus left and the Holy Spirit came down to dwell inside of the disciples, look at how strong and unwavering their faith was. Eight of the disciples were executed. They were martyrs when they died, which means that they were vocal about their belief in Christ, and never backed down when questioned. The indwelling of the Holy Spirit bolstered their spiritual strength, and they became steadfast in their faith.

The Holy Spirit is called the Comforter for a reason. He is called the Comforter because the Holy Spirit has a purpose in our lives. The Holy Spirit gives us comfort from the pain we have due to the events that have occurred in our lives. It will help us work through the traumatic and hurtful things in our lives. Instead of numbing our emotions and feelings as we used to do, we instead use the Holy Spirit to fill the holes.

That is the promise of the Holy Spirit. We no longer have to be controlled by sin. We are no longer victims of our past, nor are we merely survivors. We are instead able to thrive in all that we do. We will have ups and downs, but the Holy Spirit guarantees that we will have better lives than we had before. It will be there for us, to help us through the rough times. That is a promise I have found to be true, and it is a much better promise than any I had been made before.

Chapter 20:

From There to Here

With the Holy Spirit living inside me, my life rapidly changed as I healed and grew. A couple of months after I got sober, I felt that I was ready to be in a relationship. Sadly, I had no idea where to meet the kind of girl I wanted to date, so I decided to try out the dating website eHarmony. There, I met my amazing wife, Julie. We talked back and forth on the site through a system of questions and answers before our very first date.

Unbeknownst to me, but known by God, Julie had been orbiting just outside of my life for years. When I was living in Branson and chose to go to Hollister High School, she was attending Branson High School. When I worked at Mesquite Charlie's, she had eaten there several times and had heard my call name, Desperado, over the loudspeaker. A gifted singer, she had turned to her father and sung out the words to the song bearing that same name. It is evident that God was waiting for the precise moment to place the two of us together. Had we met before my salvation; I would have tried to drag her down with me. Although, quite frankly, she would probably have had nothing to do with me given my behavior at that time. She was and still is the polar opposite of me, the yin to my yang. She has never done drugs, never had a criminal charge, and lived a pretty amazing life. She shared my faith, although mine was newfound, and hers was a lifelong belief. She did not judge me. She saw me for who I was, not the person I used to be.

Partially to warn her that I may not be good enough for her, I laid out everything about my past very honestly for her, and she did not shy away. While I had been incredibly promiscuous, Julie had never even kissed a man. She had dated but had never accepted a second date with anyone as she never felt that they were not the right guy. It was such a blessing that she had waited on the Lord until He ordained for us to be together. Once we met, we talked every day and spent as much time together as possible.

After our very first date, Julie and I went back to her place just to talk. I chose the farthest spot away from her on the couch to sit, placing pillows as a mock wall of protection between us to ensure that no physical temptation would arise. I had slept with and used hundreds of women, but I was now different—I valued Julie's virtue and desired to protect it. A month into dating, Julie called me in tears. I tried to calm her down, finding out what was wrong. It turns out that she thought that I was going to break up with her because I hadn't even attempted to kiss her yet. She didn't know how wrong she was. When we married, we had saved sex for our wedding night, and it was amazing. I have and continue to be faithful to her. We have a fantastic relationship based on far more than carnal desires because we focused instead on friendship and respect that developed over time. I see her as a mate and partner in life instead of just an object to meet my needs. I am so much more sexually fulfilled now with my wife, than when I was an agnostic.

My wife and I had a daughter a few years after we married, and I am so thankful that my son also remains a huge part of my life. My son's mother and I have made up. We decided to put aside our differences and put our son first. She has since remarried a nice guy who already had a son and daughter of his own. I have my son one-third of the month, but a couple of times a year, my ex and her family join with my family, and we go to the local Ozarks' amusements parks together as one big family. That is what recovery can do!

In moving forward in recovery, I found some early role models that I learned a lot from, but as I grew, I noticed that so many people seemed to stagnate or settle for merely existing. As a guy that goes full throttle towards whatever it is that motivates me, I found this to be discouraging. I recognized that if I wanted to aspire to be better, then I needed to find a positive mentor. I needed someone that was a role model in all the areas that I wanted to be successful in: as a husband, a father, a Christian, an influencer, a community leader, and ultimately a world changer. I located a member of our community that I could emulate, and his example has guided me significantly. This inspired me to live a better life in recovery, but ultimately to set more substantial goals and be a catalyst for change in the recovery community as a whole.

I graduated with my master's degree in social work, initially working as a therapist and becoming a licensed clinical social worker. Recovery became my defining passion, and I now serve in a variety of ways within this field.

Today, I am the chair for the Missouri State Advisory Council on Alcohol and Drug Abuse, which under my recommendation and the vote of the council has been renamed the Missouri State Advisory Council of Substance Use Prevention and Recovery. I serve on the planning committee for the Missouri Department of Mental Health's yearly Consumer Conference, am on the Greene County Citizen's Advisory Board for Probation and Parole, and am a member of the Recovery Coalition of the Ozarks. I helped create the training for the Missouri Certified Peer Specialists, and I am one of twelve facilitators in the state. I have spoken in churches, schools, conferences, colleges, and other venues about the power of recovery as well as advocated and provided testimony in our state capital for legislation that supports recovery and people staying alive long enough to enter into recovery. I have trained thousands of people in the application of Narcan and rescue breathing. For over two years, I was the Missouri Advocacy and Education Outreach Coordinator for the Missouri Recovery Network, traveling the state. Before that, I worked for eight years at a residential and outpatient treatment center, focusing mostly on working with various treatment courts. Recovery is not just part of me, it defines me and is my passion.

In 2012, I came to the realization that what I was doing as a counselor and a member of the recovery community was not nearly enough. I wanted to do more. I felt like I was part of the recovery community, but I never felt like I was part of the community I lived in. Following in the footsteps of my mentor, I felt compelled to make a difference, so I started a non-profit called Better Life in Recovery (BLiR).

In the first year, BLiR did an event in a small community in Ash Grove, Missouri. I was invited by a pastor who felt at a loss. He said, "I have kids that are third generation methamphetamine users, and I don't know what to do." We brought in games, food, live music, and speakers with life experience to try and make a difference. It was a lot of fun, and I felt like we had an impact on a group that would usually never have been reached.

In 2013 we expanded on this, hosting three events: an event much like the one we did in Ash Grove; only this time in the larger city of Springfield, Missouri, a recovery picnic, and a float trip. Our humble beginning was already impacting the community.

In February of 2014, I was scrolling through my feed on Facebook when I chanced upon articles posted in the local newspaper and television stations discussing the passing of Phillip Seymour Hoffman. I made the mistake of reading the comments people had left:

"Who cares, just another dead junkie."

"We should give heroin away for free, so these people will eliminate themselves from the gene pool."

"He was sober for years and then started using again. These people never get better."

"Once a junkie, always a junkie."

I was saddened and sickened, and I knew that things had to change. I called local businesses, pastors, attorneys, treatment providers, and people from the various recovery fellowships and invited them to a meeting. That first meeting, we had about thirty people show up. I talked to them and told them about my goals for the future for BLiR. The mission was to deal hope and foster dignity for those who struggle with substance use and mental health issues through community service, education, and educational events that celebrate people in long-term recovery. We planned seven events for 2014. We had a 5K/10K Recovery Run, which multiple organizations contributed to. We had proclamations for Recovery Month presented by Senator Dixon for the state of Missouri and Councilman Bensch for the city of Springfield. The run was followed by a free BBQ, music, bounce houses, face painting, and other free family activities. BLiR hosted Recovery Day at Hammons Field, our local minor league ball field, which had three hundred people in attendance. To support us, State Representative Burlison threw out the first pitch, and we had a parade of people in recovery as their friends and allies surrounded the field before the game. One of our representatives sang God Bless America during the seventh-inning stretch. We partnered with Springfield Public Schools, and the recovery community painted four elementary school playgrounds. We also had a Keeping it Clean River Clean Up and Campout. Things were starting to gain momentum as we changed both the recovery community and our community as a whole.

Continuing to grow, in 2015, we held sixty-four events. We did everything that we did in 2014 and so much more. We started a stream team to clean up our waterways and had several floats. We helped area nonprofits such as our local domestic violence organization, Harmony House. We worked to help provide safety from hoarding and squalor through the organization Safe and

Sanitary Homes. In fact, we logged almost two thousand hours of community service. We started a weekly, Sunday night sober bowling event. We started having family game nights and sober karaoke parties Saturday nights and filed and received our 501(c)(3) status as a nonprofit organization.

In 2016, we again did the 5K/10K Recovery Run and Family Fun BBQ, Recovery Day at Hammons Field, and the Hootentown Keeping It Clean River Cleanup and Campout. We once again partnered with Springfield Public Schools, Harmony House, Community Partnership of the Ozarks, and other organizations to put in community impact hours. The Keeping it Clean Stream Team did six events, several with overnight campouts included. We still bowled every Sunday, doing game nights and adding paintball and laser tag outings as well.

Today, several years later, through BLiR, people in recovery and their families are vital to the community they live in. Through recovery, we are people giving back to our communities and making them better. Each year, BLiR has added one or two core people to multiply our efforts and expand. In the first several years, we operated using all volunteers, donated space, and the help of local businesses or individuals for sponsors at some of the larger events.

Along the way, something else really exciting happened. For years, I had talked about needing a home base of operations for BLiR but had gained no ground. I dreamed about having a place that would offer a one-stop-shop for those with an active substance use disorder, those in recovery, or people who care about those who have a substance use disorder, needing some questions answered or some support. Excitingly, in May of 2016, BLiR, in partnership with Jericho Commission and New Beginnings Sanctuary, opened the Springfield Recovery Community Center (SRCC). We worked hard to set it up, working together and pooling our resources and contacts. During National Recovery Month in September of that same year, we had the official grand opening.

Instantly, BLiR had a brick and mortar location to host events. We continued doing sober karaoke parties, movies, and game nights. We added pool tables, dart boards, televisions, gaming systems, and bookcases stocked with books. We also began having support groups for those with substance use disorders but also for their family and friends. We did Springfield's first public Narcan training as soon as the 3rd party access bill passed into effect. In 2018 we had over 800 groups and events that were attended by over 14,000 people. We are making a difference, not just for those in recovery but for the entire Springfield area community!

Our influence continues to grow in not only our community but also in our state and nation as our members teach others that they too can find success in recovery. Through an application I wrote through BLiR, Springfield was one of only fifteen pilot communities for the Community Projects. I am blessed to lead the charge in my community and beyond. These changes in how we view and address recovery are impactful, and in 2017 I was recognized for my work in this field by receiving the Missouri Mental Health Champion Award.

In 2018, I was recognized by the Substance Abuse and Mental Health Services (SAMSHA) with a Voice Award given to "recognize community and entertainment leaders for elevating awareness about mental health and addiction treatment, support, and recovery." It was a tremendous honor to be flown out to Los Angeles for this event and was further evidence of how drastically my life has changed in recovery. The Voice Awards that year were hosted by Rick and Kay Warren, and it was a blessing to share the impact Celebrate Recovery has had in my life with them.

Recently I was privileged to be chosen as one of 150 recovery leaders nationwide to take part in Mobilize Recovery, a project of the Facebook Community Leadership Program and the Voices Project. As I continue to expand my reach as a keynote speaker, it is exciting to meet with other leaders and influencers to see how together we can all be more successful in reaching people through recovery.

In coordination with what I have tagged as the #hopedealer movement, we also created and presented a documentary entitled *Not My Child*. We have successfully presented this film in various communities, opening the dialogue to exploring different paths to recovery and examining the disease of addiction. Addiction affects nearly everyone in some form, and this film is being used to stimulate positive discussion and erase the stigma surrounding substance use and addiction.

This is not a complete list of all that I have done in the recovery community or continue to do. It is instead a snapshot of what can be achieved in recovery and some of the positive ways that you can be involved in being part of the solution in your own area through similar endeavors or initiatives. I say all of this to let you know a little bit about me and who I have become since that day that I gave my life completely to Christ.

Substance use changed my life for my detriment, and recovery has changed my life for the better. I say this because I want everybody to know that not only is recovery possible, it is fun and amazing. Recovery rocks! Do you want to learn the principles for recovery that have been life-changing for me and can have a similar outcome for you? Keep reading as I share the things that helped me attain long-term recovery and build the life I have today.

Part Two

Chapter 21:

Five Seconds to Make a Good Impression

"Hi, my name is David, and I am a person in long-term recovery. What that means for me is that I have not used alcohol or other drugs since the thirty-first of January in 2009, and because of that, I have been able to do some amazing things in my community that I would love to talk to you about."

That is my elevator speech. That is how I introduce myself when I speak. My identity lies in my recovery, not my addiction. Don't get me wrong, I appreciate my past. The experiences I had helped to shape me into the person I am today, but at the same time, they do not describe the person I am today.

Early in my sobriety, I reveled in my past. I had used drugs or alcohol from the age of twelve to thirty-six, so I had no other experiences in which to take pride. I took pride in being a tough guy who was the biggest dealer around, sleeping with the hottest girls, and doing more drugs or drinking more alcohol than everyone else.

Initially, my testimony was seventy-five percent war and twenty-five percent sobriety, and that twenty-five percent is probably a gross overestimation. Because of that, I still thought of myself as a thug, a convict, and a junkie. I was a recovering addict and alcoholic. That was who I was at that time. I still hung on to most of my character defects, which led me back to relapse again and again. *I'm not who I was.*

My addiction laid my foundation, but recovery is what was built upon it. That is what people see today. It is the image that I want to remain in people's minds. Some people have an issue with this. I have had people from various organizations tell me that I am forgetting my past when I identify myself this way. I promise I have not forgotten my past. I refer to not doing drugs or alcohol, letting them know what I am in recovery from. The difference is that the mental picture it draws is different.

It is positive for me, and it paints a more precise picture when I introduce myself that way. If I say I am a grateful recovering addict, many people in the community visualize me sitting on the corner of a bed with my arm tied off, getting ready to put a needle in my arm. If I say I am a recovering alcoholic, they imagine me passed out in an alley next to a bottle of Ripple. This is not the image I want people to have when I am striving to be one of the faces of recovery and trying to change the stigma around recovery. Instead, I want them to see me for who I am today. I have been transformed.

Today, I am in long-term recovery. I am a hope dealer. I am a stigma killer. I am a public speaker. I am a motivator!

There is a better life in recovery. I am living proof, and there are another 23.5 million of us in recovery in the United States. If we all stand and shout the wonders of recovery in our communities, the stigma will fade into nonexistence.

Join the movement, and together we will change the face of recovery. It starts with these eleven words:

Hi, my name is _____ and I am in long-term recovery!

Chapter 22:

I'm Not Okay, And I'm Okay With That

When I first got sober, I could not stand myself. Every time that I looked into the mirror, all I could say about the guy staring back was that he was an addict, junkie, convict, and a horrible person. I knew that there were so many people out there that were better than I would ever be, and because of that, my self-esteem, self-confidence, and self-image were horrible.

I knew that deep down, I was not okay, and I hated that. I was not just riddled with guilt about my past, I was drowning in shame about my present. I could not see any reason that anyone would like me. I knew that I did not want to go back to prison, so I, in turn, stopped doing drugs and started drinking. I quit drugs, but then gradually instead became an alcoholic with rage issues. I measured my scale of happiness based on the person I was currently sleeping with.

Using alcohol, I tried to numb myself and escape from my past, justifying my constant drunkenness by assuring myself that this method of escape was far more socially acceptable and mainstream than the methamphetamines and opiates I had once used. The problem was that I was still trapped in my addiction--it had just changed names. I had shifted addictions several times, converting my need for drugs, sex, violence, money, and power to only alcohol, anger, and sex, which in my mind somehow justified things. At the time, I honestly thought this was an improvement. Once I met Jesus, I shifted to sobriety and food. The sobriety part is excellent, but addiction to food can be just as problematic as any other addiction. Therefore, I am still working on my comfort eating, and it is a constant struggle.

The real problem wasn't just accepting myself for who I am today instead of who I once was, but forgiving myself for the choices I had once made. I thought that sobriety was like a magical cure. No one ever told me that it was not. When I would get sober, I would initially be happy and content. These feelings would satisfy me for a while, but would eventually always sour over time. I would spend a month or so listening to people relive their "glory days" in their addictions while bemoaning how miserable their current lives were, in comparison, now that they were clean and sober.

After complaining about all the struggles living their life today, they would then inevitable include the hollow-sounding disclaimer that sobriety was "still better than life used to be. I'm not where I want to be, but thank God I'm not where I was." This statement seemed empty because no one ever regaled the meeting with the joys of sober living--they always seemed to be happiest when sharing their war stories of the past. This never sat right with me, so I would go back out and resume my old behavior. If there was no real hope for relief from my misery, why would I want to clean up at all?

I had also done horrible things in my life that I could not forgive myself for, and this clouded my view of myself. I kept seeing who I was and not who God created me to be. So, I always sabotaged myself. Making amends from people in my past and present was the easy part. I was a chameleon, a convincing liar. You can lie to other people, but you can't hide the truth from yourself. The problem was that when I looked in the mirror, the man looking back knew the truth about me, and I could not convince myself that I was a good person like some of the truly genuine people that God has placed in my life.

I thought that recovery was all about building a new life, putting the past behind you, and living the fulfilling life that "normal" people live. It took me a while to discover that all of that was not true. Here are some things that led to me having a better outlook on my life:

1. I should never compare myself to anyone else. If I know one thing, it is that I would make a horrible anyone else. I can make the best version of myself possible, so that is my goal.

2. I have a substance use disorder and will always have a substance use disorder, it's just in remission. That is not a bad thing; it just means that I cannot use drugs or alcohol responsibly and they will therefore not be used by me...ever

3. Life is not all rainbows and cotton candy. Life is lollipops, and lemon drops. There is full of moments both sweet and sour, happy and sad, positive and negative--not just for you but for everyone. Whether it is the best or worst day you have ever had, it will soon pass.

4. No one is genuinely okay all the time. Everyone has problems, there is no perfect person. They do not exist. You can, however, have a perfectly normal life once you realize that life is not perfectly normal.

5. Every one of my past mistakes or traumas has given me both wisdom and strength. I would not be who I am today if not for every single event that I have ever lived through.

6. I embrace the positives AND negatives. They all have led me to where I am today, and I like where I am at.

7. The world is imperfect, so it stands to reason that the people in it have imperfections. I am one of those imperfect people.

There is perfection in me. Christ is perfection in me. I was made to be the best possible version of myself that I can be. I have come to realize that I am shattered…perfectly shattered. These realizations led me to one conclusion that no one is truly, "okay." When we accept this to be true, it helps us to move forward in becoming who God made us to be.

Throughout my life, I have been friends with some talented people: inventors, doctors, counselors, pastors, scientists, etc. I have also been friends with some people who were well off financially: politicians, lawyers, trust fund kids, business owners, etc. I have also been friends with people with substance use disorders, people who were convicted of heinous felonies, homeless people, and those working for minimum wage. All these different individuals from varying walks of life had some things in common. Every single one of them had days that they were happy and days that they were depressed. At times they felt self-worthy, and at other times they each lacked self-esteem. One day they might feel successful, just to wake up the next day feeling like they had not lived up to their potential. In the end, no one I have ever met was perfect.

In fact, in all my life, I have only read about one perfect person, and it was not you or me…it was Jesus Christ. He was perfect, yet this didn't make him immune from the trials and pain of the world that we live in. I realized that no one is okay, twenty-four-seven. I am just as imperfect as everyone else on this planet. It took me a long time to be able to say this, but here goes. I AM NOT OKAY, and I am okay with that!

Chapter 23:

Healed People Heal People

I am sure you know the saying, "Hurt people hurt people." This simply means that when people are hurting, they tend to lash out and hurt other people. Sometimes, it may be unintentional. You may have spent your workday hearing your boss jump all over you like he was a ten-year-old in a bounce house, only to get home and take your own stress out by snapping at your own family. It could be more intentional. Maybe like I was, you are getting abused at home by someone so you go to school and bully kids weaker than you so you can feel a sense of control or power. It could also be completely intentional. You are hurt by a loved one who pushes your buttons, so you retaliate by pushing their buttons.

I used to look at my grandfather with nothing but hatred, but over time I was able to see that in his own way, he was just a hurting individual. Maybe it was something that occurred while he served in the military in World War II, or perhaps he was abused and mistreated himself, but at some point, my grandpa experienced his own hurt. I am not sure how or what, but something in his past devastated him, and he never got over it. Instead of healing, his mission became making other people as miserable as he was. Over time, he got to be really good at it. He never found healing from his hurts. Instead, he used alcohol, tobacco, work, and angry evil acts to mask the hurts of his past. The problem was that since he never healed from these hurts, they never got any better. As soon as the rush was over from abusing someone, all of his past problems would come back. Then, he would have to do something evil again to numb or escape his past.

It is a shame he never tried to face his demons. If he had overcome them, there would have been significant changes, not just in him but in the people he interacted with. His life and the lives of those he came into contact with could have been different. If he had focused on healing for himself, the rage and anger would not have been there, and he would not have hurt others, taking out his emotions on them.

If hurt people hurt people, then the opposite is true as well. Healed people heal people. Once someone overcomes something, they have a unique insight into that experience that other people don't have. For example, I spent twenty-five years of my life floundering in addiction. I have now been in recovery for over ten years. I know what it takes to stop using and build an amazing life. I can share what has helped me, what methods I have seen help others, and the science that has validated some forms of treatment, so they are recognized as effective evidence-based practices.

I have several close friends that have been diagnosed with cancer and after treatment are now either cancer-free or in remission. They have unique perspectives that I lack. One: they have been diagnosed with cancer. I have no idea what that feels like to be diagnosed with cancer. I have never had cancer, so although I can have empathy and support someone who has cancer, my friends come from a place of wisdom and experience that I lack. Second: they have overcome that cancer through treatment. They are living proof that surviving a cancer diagnosis is not only possible but a reality because of this firsthand knowledge. They can give hope and encourage people that I cannot because they have lived through cancer.

Everyone has been through something. We all have been hurt in one way or another. It could be physical abuse, sexual abuse, feeling fat, being told we are worthless, being bullied, depression, cancer, being a child of someone with a substance use disorder, grief, and loss, etc. I am sure you get the idea. There are a lot of ways that life hurts us.

Life puts holes in our souls. Once those holes are placed, many of us use something to escape, numb, or forget the hole is there. Food, sex, money, cutting, power, alcohol, and other drugs are a few of the things we use as Band-Aids to numb or escape from our past. These bandages don't heal the problem, they just cover them up. They are still festering underneath, while more issues are being added to it.

Fortunately, some of us have figured out how to stop covering the problem up. We have learned what it takes to fix the problem. Once we learned how to deal with the holes instead of running from them, we have unique wisdom that only someone who has gone through what we have experienced has. Once we have that wisdom, we can impart it to others. That is all part of what I call my garbage theory and the concept of spiritual spackle, which I discuss later in subsequent chapters.

Many people live with regrets about their past choices and things that have happened to them. I have learned to embrace mine. I am not defined by them. Instead, I define myself by my recovery. I realize that all those events led me to be the person I am today. The person that I am today helps people. It is were not for everything I have been through and experienced; I would lack effectiveness in doing that.

The same is true for you. Everyone has survived or lived through something that had an impact on them. Never forget that the past has made you who you are, and the person you are today is incredible, and with continued growth and healing will only get better with time. To quote a jazz singer from many years ago, "My God don't make no junk." You are not junk, and there is no reason to let your past issues define you. My past did not defeat me; it made me stronger and wiser than I ever would have been without it. The same is true for you!

Chapter 24:

Why I was Depressed

Now if there's a smile on my face
It's only there trying to fool the public
But when it comes down to fooling you
Now honey that's quite a different subject
But don't let my glad expression
Give you the wrong impression
Really I'm sad, oh sadder than sad
You're gone and I'm hurting so bad
Like a clown I pretend to be glad
Now there's some sad things known to man
But ain't too much sadder than
the tears of a clown
When there's no one around
Smokey Robinson - The Tears of a Clown

In my addiction, my hopelessness and depression reached abysmal depths. I got so that low I attempted suicide. If my sister hadn't found me unconscious in a pool of blood, I would not be here. She saved my life. Not that I would call what I had then a life.

When you spend six days awake on methamphetamine, sleeping only one day per week, you are not really living. However, back then, if you would have cared to ask, I would have told you otherwise. I would have told you I was "fine." In my life, FINE stood for Fearful, Insecure, Numb, and Emotional.

Fearful- I was afraid that I would never stop using drugs. I was also scared that my life was never going to get any better. I was terrified that when I died, I would turn to dust, so nothing that I ever did mattered. I was horrified that I had let down my family and would never do anything that they could be proud of me for. That fear turned outward and was expressed as rage. I was violent and angry in hopes that no one would get close to me. I did not want to give people the chance to hurt me again, so I stopped caring about anyone and anything but myself and my next fix.

Insecure- I knew that other people had not been beaten as I had, but that was at least something that I felt that I could share with others. I knew that other guys had not been molested like I had and therefore was so afraid of what people would think about me if they knew. I was depressed all of the time and felt weak and soft.

Numb- This is what a lot of my drug use was--a numbing agent. I never wanted to be hurt again emotionally or psychologically, and staying high was a great way to ensure that no one could get close. If my focus was on getting high, I developed no close relationships. Staying spun allowed me to feel nothing. Avoiding authentic relationships and preventing myself from feeling emotions was the perfect storm for creating the numb condition I desired.

Emotional- I would cry when I was by myself. I could feel alone in my house, even surrounded by ten other people or at a club that contained hundreds. I was depressed to levels that no one should ever have to live with. Other times, I was so angry that the littlest thing would cause me to erupt. I would put holes in walls and hit people for no reason, other than the fact that I did not like who I was and what I had become. I was so unhappy in my own skin, and nothing I did changed that.

As for the suicide, that would not be the last time I tried to kill myself. No, I was sure that there was no hope of sobriety in my future, and my addiction was wearing me down. It had not even taken me two years of using drugs IV, to realize that life sucked. Beyond that, I only knew one thing, my life was only going to get worse.

Even though I promised my sister that I would never try to kill myself again, I lied. My annual Russian roulette games were evidence of that. I would attempt suicide, in this manner, multiple times. It would happen on my birthday or a couple of times after really long meth runs when I didn't sleep for weeks and was utterly spent. Emptying my revolver of all but one bullet, then spinning the cylinder and placing the cold muzzle of the gun to my head became a ritual for me. The sound of the hammer clicking, so shockingly loud to my ears. I would feel angry that the gun didn't go off, ending my pain, yet would simultaneously be awash in relief. I was conflicted about whether or not I wanted to live or die, so I gambled on the spin of the revolver.

People who struggle with addictions can justify anything, even making decisions that they really don't want to. It wasn't that I wanted to die. I just knew that I could not go on living my life the way I was. I was so tired, hopeless, and depressed. I always covered it up so well that no one knew. As referenced in the song, I put on the mask of the clown, laughing and joyous on the outside.

In this, I was an amazing actor. I had built up walls in my youth that I hid behind, and no one was ever allowed to see the real me. The foundation for those walls began when I was only three or four years old, experiencing the abuse from my babysitter. As my walls grew bigger, so did my ability to show people only what I wanted them to see. They saw happy, popular, outgoing me. This could not have been further from the truth of what I held inside.

I was depressed all of the time. I looked around and saw how happy the people I partied with seemed, and I knew that there must be something wrong with me. How come I was not happy?

Why did I not feel motivated to do anything unless I got high? Why did I feel so alone while they all seemed to be living it up?

The lie most people hear is that people are addicted to drugs and alcohol because it makes them feel great. For me, though, it may have started that way, the last few years that could not have been further from the truth. I was no longer using to feel good. I was using to feel not quite as bad. My life was miserable each and every day. I did not have the motivation to leave the house, and if I went to sleep, I couldn't get out of bed and function unless I got high. It wasn't about feeling good, it was simply about trying not to feel so bad.

Today, I realize that most of the people I partied with back then were depressed as well. Most of the clients that I have worked with over the years are just as miserable as I was. They, too, are hiding behind walls they have erected, never showing people the real them. That makes you even more miserable. You will never be happy when you fear what others may think or how they would react if they knew the truth of what you were hiding. Shame casts a strong shadow that is hard to step out from under.

You can never be yourself if you are terrified that people will either judge you or see you as weak and use your vulnerabilities against you. Most of us have learned how to read people and act accordingly. For me, this mostly began with learning to predict and respond to my grandpa. The babysitter taught me how to hide how I was feeling, the chaos of my parents' relationship taught me how to blend in dependent on the situation, but my grandpa taught me that you had to read people to attempt to avoid abuse and hate.

Now that I have studied the science of addiction, it has shed even more light on why I was so depressed. I will try to explain this in the simplest way possible, without getting too deep into the science of it.

The nerve cells in our brain act as a communication system by receiving, sending, and processing information. Drugs disrupt that communication by either overstimulation of the reward circuits of the brain or by masquerading as naturally occurring chemical messengers in the brain.

Opiates and marijuana are the spies, infiltrating the brain by confusing the receptors and then sending abnormal messages by activating nerve cells. Stimulants, on the other hand, either prevent brain cells from recycling neurotransmitters or cause them to release tremendous amounts of neurotransmitters, particularly dopamine.

I will focus on the amphetamines because they saturate the brain with dopamine. Dopamine controls many things, but our focus on how it impacts motivation, feelings of pleasure, and emotion. Simply put, dopamine makes us feel good. We have tremendous amounts of neurotransmitters released, which makes us feel amazing, and in turn, our brain teaches us to continue doing whatever it was that causes the euphoric effect.

I became behaviorally conditioned to do drugs because they over-stimulated the chemicals in my brain that makes me feel not just good but great! That sounds amazing, and honestly, at first, it really was. I could escape my past, my depression, and my trauma by flooding my brain with dopamine. At the time, I thought, "Who wouldn't want this?"

I had no way of predicting where the chemical process would soon lead me. Over time, the brain gets used to the intense amounts of dopamine being released and begins to reduce the number of dopamine receptors and produce less dopamine. That means that I could no longer feel happy, joyous, and free like an average person because my brain had begun rewiring itself. Not only that, but the number of drugs needed to make me feel what I used to feel has to be continually increased. They call this tolerance.

That is just how dopamine responds. We also have other neurotransmitters that are impacted over time: serotonin, norepinephrine, GABA, and glutamate, to name a few. Those of us who have used drugs have depleted levels of the feel-good, behavior control, memory, decision making, motivation, and pleasure producing chemicals in our brain. The only way we can even come close to feeling normal emotions is to take more and more of the drugs we are using. That is why we use, and that is why I found myself mired in my substance abuse.

The truth is...that I was not happy. I was miserable ALL OF THE TIME.

Using no longer made me feel the same feelings I once had. Chasing the high had dropped me to new lows. I had to take more and more drugs simply to maintain. That is what they call chasing the dragon, trying to find that same high you once had. I could only get the same feeling, if not a better feeling, from using a little bit more and a little bit more over the years. Then the drugs stopped working that way. They started having increasingly less of an impact on my mood and motivation.

I woke up in the morning after sleeping with no desire to get out of bed, swallowed in a well of depression. I could never quite get out of the well, but I could pull myself up to the top and at least see the sun. Using took the edge off. It did not make me feel euphoric like it once had, but it made me feel a little bit better. I had depleted levels of neurotransmitters in my brain. That is why I was depressed all of the time. In the end, using made me feel slightly less awful, and that was enough to keep me continuously using despite all of the negative consequences substance use had on my life.

Today, I have found happiness. I have found a better life in recovery. My journey ultimately resulted in a drastic spiritual intervention that led to my transformation. Your journey to recovery may look different, and that is okay. There are many different paths to recovery, and my journey may look completely different from yours. However, I want to share some things that have helped me along the way.

In the subsequent chapters, you will learn my *Platinum Rule* along with the *Three Questions That Changed My Life*. Applying these principles with *The Locker Room* to your life will make a massive difference in your recovery. These are all things that I did and have seen many others successfully do, and we have attained long-term recovery.

Additionally, here are some tips to help you in your recovery:

- Don't just focus on taking negative people, places, and things out of your life. Instead, continually add positive people, places, and things to it, replacing the negatives instead of leaving a void. The negatives will be forced out due to the positives smothering and suffocating them. The positives you add will usurp the negatives. Slowly but surely, making positive choices will become second nature because they will create new neural pathways.

- Never sell yourself short; you, too, can find happiness. It does not happen all at once, but it WILL happen.

- It takes time.

- As I have heard, many people say, "Don't leave before the miracle happens."

YES, YOU CAN!!!

Chapter 25:

Grateful for my Past

I often used to wonder what would have happened if I had not taken a walk that night long ago in Highland? What if I would have stayed inside like my dad had asked, never visiting the square and meeting the people I would experience my first drug use with? What if I had reported to my probation officer instead of going on the run or going to prison? What if I didn't drink or drive the night I wrecked and died three times, eventually leading me to my introduction to opiates?

I have learned through experience that you can what-if the past all you want to, yet all it will do is waste your time. It will never change what happened. Beating yourself up about the past is time that could be better spent improving yourself in the present. The fact remains, I took a walk that day and bumped into a kid who introduced me to a few more kids, and ultimately those choices changed me forever. Every decision I have ever made is something that I cannot take back.

Have you ever wondered, "When will I feel or be the person that I used to be?" It could be because you struggle with addiction, you lived through a natural disaster, you were abused as a child, or you lost a child. You want to get over it, to forget it and move on. You want to forget that it happened so that your life can return to normal. I often have people that I work with ask me the same question, "When do I get to be the person that I was before this happened?"

The short answer is simple, NEVER! Before you shut me out, hear me out. You have read how I was abused as a child, my parents separated, and I blamed myself. I went to prison, dealt drugs, attempted suicide, and I was involved in manufacturing methamphetamine. I was addicted to drugs and alcohol. There is nothing that I can ever do to change what I did in the past. No time machine to hop in and undo what I have already done.

Along the way, I found that no amount of anger, anxiety, self-loathing, denial, depression, bargaining, or escape will change my past. I wasted a lot of energy on that in my past, yet everything that I had done remained done. I never was able to change the choices I made before. I beat myself up for years about it. I hated myself! Every time that I looked into a mirror, I saw a convict, a junkie, and a dope cook. I was miserable, and I saw no way of ever escaping my past. I had not shot up in a decade, but I still thought about it sometimes, and I judged myself for doing it.

Then I heard an example that changed my life. I will share it with you now, and in the manner that I share it with others. The analogy is this: we are all born cucumbers. This is not a bad thing as there is nothing wrong with a cucumber. It may be a little bland and tasteless, but it still has a purpose. However, I cannot eat a cucumber all by itself. I generally need to dip it in ranch dressing or eat it with other things in a salad. It is food, but it lacks flavor.

Now, take that cucumber and add some spices and vinegar. Then let it soak all that up and simmer it for a while until it is fully saturated. Over time that cucumber changes and becomes something different; you have a delicious pickle. That bland, ordinary cucumber has been transformed into something awesome! Just as we, as humans, are transformed by the things we experience and overcome in our lives. We soak in all of the negative things that happen to us, whether they are done by others or by our choice, then use those to change us.

Before my addiction, I was a cucumber, now I am a pickle. I have more flavor, so to speak. Thanks to my substance use disorder, mental health diagnosis, and years of trauma, I have gained strength and wisdom that can only be obtained through overcoming! Without my past, I am just like everybody else. I am normal. That is not a bad thing, the world needs normal people. That said, the world also needs the rest of us. We pickles serve a fantastic function. Who better to help someone overcome addiction than someone who used to be there themselves? Who better to give hope to someone battling depression than someone who has fought depression?

I do my job as well as I do, for two reasons. One reason is that I have gone through extensive training in college and continuing educational training. I have read countless books and listened to multiple experts in the field. I use evidence-based practices to help those I come in contact with. The second reason is that I also have lived as an addict, and by the grace of God, I overcame my addictions. That gives me empathy that many do not have. It has allowed me to stay positive and hopeful when working with clients and friends who are struggling with life-controlling issues.

In the ministry, Celebrate Recovery, we call these issues hurts, habits, and hang-ups. We do that because it does not just have to be an addiction. In fact, addiction seldom exists in isolation. I was abused, molested, raped, abandoned, beaten, from a broken family, and struggled with mental health issues, etc. The list goes on as I experienced trauma after trauma. Recovery is working through all of those issues and finding that a better life exists.

Without the history of my past, some people that I help by relating to them would not be reached. They would not find hope through working with me if they could not connect to me. Research shows that the therapeutic alliance is the single most important indicator of success! People don't care how much you know until they know how much you care! I can build that alliance because I am a pickle. Someone in the pickling process can talk to me or hear my story and know that they, too, can eventually step out of their addiction. As for pickles, we can impart hope to those who are still struggling that one day, they also can be a pickle! Our past flavors our present with experience and knowledge that we would not otherwise have.

Now, if you wanted to take that pickle and turn it back into a cucumber, could you do it? Of course not, once a cucumber is pickled, it can never be unpickled. It has now undergone a permanent change and become something totally different. That said, why would it ever want to be a cucumber again? Now that I have some flavor (experience, wisdom, and strength), why would I want to give that up?

When I think of people who save others' lives, there is a list that comes to my mind. I think of firefighters, nurses, doctors, paramedics, and hope dealers in recovery. All of those people have had to go through specialized training to save others. Some people go to college or an academy to learn how to save lives. We lived life, and then through the twelve steps, Christ, or some other pathway, we have overcome our issues, and now we are willing to share our strength, experience, and hope with others.

Since I have begun to use my past to empower others, I have come to peace with my history. I went from dealing dope to dealing hope, and I would never change what I do today. Not only can I talk to people with active substance use disorders, but I also have the privilege of talking to pastors, chaplains, missionaries, college students, professors, counselors, probation officers, and the families and parents who are impacted. Your life can become amazing, not in spite of your past, but because of it. In recovery, we do great things!

Chapter 26:

Good Enough Ain't Good Enough Anymore

In my addiction, I usually did the wrong thing. On occasion, I would do the right thing. Sometimes it was because I still had some remaining principles; other times, it was so that I could bring it up later to explain or justify why I was not quite as bad as other people. Most of the time, it was by blind luck. Even a broken watch is right twice a day. Needless to say, I thought the life that I was living in my addiction was good enough. I felt that what I was doing was good enough to keep doing until it wasn't, which took about seventeen years...then an additional seven.

Only when my probation officer caught me using, and I was facing the ten-year back-up, did I decided to get sober. I didn't honestly do it for myself, but I had been busted and figured that rehab was better than prison. I was not doing it for me or to truly change, I did it to avoid the consequence of prison. In a sense, I also did it to show other people that I was not who they thought I was. I thought my reasoning was good enough, but my sobriety only lasted a couple of months before I relapsed.

When I tried to get sober a year later, I never really pushed myself. Instead, I would just do enough to get by. I was excellent at faking it. I overachieved at the goals others set for me but never really had any goals for myself. Even when I did the one-hundred-fifty meetings in ninety days far exceeding the ninety meetings in ninety days benchmark, I never really listened while I was there. I was too busy telling people all that I knew about sobriety, which, after three months of attending meetings, could have fit inside a thimble. I would also join in on the war stories and bragging, which a lot of other people there liked to listen to. I was regularly drinking, but I was no longer using opioids and meth. Still, I thought that what I was doing was good enough until it no longer helped.

I had a counselor who told me not to do drugs, and that alcohol was a drug, so I followed in his footsteps and was sober for a month. I actually looked up to him and respected him. Then one day, he came into the restaurant I worked at and sat at the bar. While he was at the bar, he had several alcoholic drinks. He obviously thought that no one could see him, or that he didn't have a drinking problem. I am not sure which it was because I never saw him again. For him, what he was doing was good enough. I went out that night and got drunk. If he could do it, so could I. Was he the reason I drank? No, but he was a reason that I used. It was good enough.

When I quit using drugs that were illegal and switched to alcohol, I justified it because alcohol was legal. I could rationalize my drinking all day long. Even though I would blackout most every night, I still worked and went to college. I also managed to graduate with honors. I was an alcoholic that drank and drove multiple times EVERY NIGHT. I would wake up with no idea how I got home. I would wake up with shakes and drink to make them go away. Was I happy? No, I was miserable, but in my eyes, I was good enough.

Then I decided I wanted more. I wanted more for my life, my son's life, my relationships, my employment, my day to day life. I was no longer happy with what I had. It was not enough. Good was not enough. I wanted to attain greatness. I went full force in everything that I did. I decided to never settle for anything less than amazing for myself, my faith, my recovery, my wife, and my children. Good was simply not good enough anymore. I wanted great!

I found that if I wanted to change, there were things I had to realize if I wanted to live a better life:

1. Complacency kills. I wanted to be great and to do that, I could never settle. If I meet my goals, then I create new ones. I was not born to do good things; I was born to achieve greatness!

2. Keep moving. If you are not moving forward, you are moving backward. Life is a journey, not a destination.

3. Educate yourself. Learn, learn, and then learn some more. Read, have discourse with intelligent and wise people. To die ignorant is the greatest sin we can commit against ourselves.

4. Ask questions. That is the only way you can find out some things, so don't be afraid to ask. The only stupid question is the one that isn't asked.

5. Be altruistic. It really is better to give than to receive. Do for others, then do some more. There is nothing that makes me feel better than knowing I am necessary.

6. Speak loudly. When it comes to your testimony, shout it from the rooftops. After all, you are the expert in your life, there is a lot of hope and strength others can gather from this.

7. Shame sucks. Never be ashamed of who you are and what you have done. After all, these things made you the person you are today, and that person is awesome!

8. Be proud of your successes. Defeats build us, and our victories define us. Take pride in what you have accomplished. Toot your own horn and celebrate your accomplishments because other people might not. People need to hear about your wins and your losses to know who you are and what you are about. Take pride in the positive things you do.

9. Be grateful. Learning the difference between wants and needs was vital to my finding happiness and a better life. There are things that I want, and there are things that I need. If I focus on my wants, I lose my ability to focus on that which is essential. Start your day with a gratitude list and focus on what you have instead of what you don't. It makes my mornings start off well, which impacts the rest of my day.

10. Never surrender. I was beaten so many times before I even tried because I listened to the voice that told me I could not do it. I stopped listening to that voice and accepted I had no limitations as long as I was not dead. That is when the game is over. If you are still breathing, then victory can still be yours!

11. Learn and live The Locker Room. This is critical for recovery success, and I have included an entire chapter outlining this principle for you.

12. Put God first. My life is no longer about me. I put God first, and everything else comes second. If I put God first, it makes all other areas of my life better. I become a better husband, father, friend, employee, etc. It all starts with

God and trickles down from there. After all, I was an addict for decades and tried every way you can imagine to quit using and failed. As an atheist, I said a fox hole prayer a decade ago, and I have not used since then. I am way happier as a result!

Chapter 27:

The Three Questions That Changed My Life

Does this sound too easy to you--just one rule, consisting of asking yourself three questions that can change your life? I am sure that it seems too good and too simple to be true. Is there really one rule that can help me to change the way that I live my life if I apply it? I say, yes! I am living proof that you can make changes in life, no matter where you once were. I have been through the wringer over and over again. I hit rock bottom, then I grabbed a shovel, as most of us do. It is as if hitting bottom is not good enough for many of us in our addictions.

I always thought that being bad was all that I was good at. I tried to be an overachiever in my addiction, from drugs to violence to sex to crime. When I realized that I needed to make changes after I got saved, I made just one change. Mind you, it was one significant change that I made in my life, and it was always applied. That one thing was to ask myself several questions before I did anything. It turns out that I am a first thought-wrong thought kind of guy (maybe first five or so thoughts wrong).

If I wanted to do something, it was probably not the right thing to do, because my instincts were awful. To counteract that, I found several questions that I could ask myself that would assist me in making the right decision. In time, I found that it was all I needed to do. After a while, I no longer had to ask myself these questions as I learned and grew. The same will be true for you. It will not happen overnight for most of us, but eventually, we will not need to ask ourselves the questions anymore. Why? We will no longer have to live our lives as if we have to answer the question each time because the question that we used to ask ourselves will be answered. We will have developed a pattern of doing the right thing. How do we develop that pattern?

To start off with, we will look at how a pattern is made. Imagine that you live in a house that is separated by several hundred yards of woods from your best friend's house. Furthermore, imagine that it is quicker to cut through the woods than to go around them considering the shortest path between two places is a straight line. Visualize yourself going through the woods. The first time that you go through those woods, it will be difficult. You will have to walk through briars and overgrown brush. You will have to try to blaze a new trail. The next day, you will have to pay careful attention to the path so that you can see it--if you can see it at all. As the days pass and you and your friend are walking back and forth through the woods several times a day, the trail through the woods will begin to get trampled down. It will become more accessible and easier to get through the woods to your best friend's house, and staying on the right path won't be as difficult. That path will get easier to see. Eventually, you will have a nice trail, and the danger of the briars and brush will be gone. You will now be able to stay on the path with very little attention to it because it is well-worn and obvious.

Our brain acts in much the same way. We have electrical impulses in our brain that are sent from neuron to neuron, much like the path from your house to your best friend's house in the illustration. These electrical impulses begin to build neural pathways in the synapses between our neurons. The neural pathways are the trails that we talked about as we walk to our best friend's house, and the synapses are the woods that separate the two houses. These trails are presently nonexistent for some of us. We have never done the right thing. If we did, it was probably accidental or incidental. We, therefore, have our work cut out for us.

At first, we have pathways that have already been built that we will have to overcome. It may seem almost automatic for us to scream or fight when we get angry. When we need something, our first impulse may be to steal it or hustle to make money illegally instead of working for it. When we are offered a drink or a drug, it is an automatic reaction to accept it. When faced with whether or not we should lie or tell the truth, we always choose to lie. We will have to overcome these first. That is why we have the questions that we will ask ourselves, any time that we are faced with having to make a decision in every situation in our life. These questions are kind of like moral training wheels for us until we forge a new trail.

As we begin to make the right choices, we create new pathways that will override the old channels we have that are wired to do the wrong thing. The more that we do the right thing, the easier it will become. Just like that trail, we will have to pay less and less attention to what we are doing because it will become a well-walked path that is now the only viable pathway for our brain's electrical impulses to travel.

What are the questions that we need to ask ourselves? For me, I realized that it was an automatic response for me to do the wrong thing. I found myself always in fights, drunk, being immoral, cursing, lying, etc. You name the sin, and I was doing it. I always justified what I was doing by saying that as long as I was not shooting up drugs, I was doing great. This seemed fine when I was agnostic and not yet a father. I had no higher power to answer to. I had no one who looked up to me that I needed to set an example for. At least that was what I thought. When I reflect back, I still had a niece that was being raised alone by my sister that needed to see what a positive male looked like. For several years, I failed her. In my anger, I was oblivious to anyone's needs other than my own.

Then I had my son, and my thinking began to change and carefully examine my life. I began to realize that I needed to make some changes in my life. I tried, and I found that I was unable to do it. Then my father died. I was lost. I could not see up from down. My drinking intensified, and I was emotionally unavailable for several months. Then I started to go to church a little more frequently, and I finally began to realize that I needed to change. I was unsure about how to do it. My brain was always hardwired to have the first-thought-wrong syndrome. I might argue that it was every-thought-wrong back then. I began to ask myself several questions that made all of the difference to me. I wanted to be a better father for my son and a better uncle for my niece, so I needed to start sooner than later. What could I possibly do to accomplish better parenting?

Over time, the best way I have found to parent is to always act like my son is on my right side and Christ is on my left. I would ask myself, "If Christ were here, would I say or do that?" and if the answer were yes, I would then ask myself, "If my son were here, would I say or do that?" This was followed by, "Would I want my son to say or do that?" If the answer to all three of those questions was yes, then I knew that it was okay to do.

As my walk forward progressed, and I began to step into recovery, I no longer had to ask myself those questions. I knew for a fact that Christ was always by my side. There was no need to pretend anymore. Furthermore, I did not need to ask myself if my son were there, "would I do this?" After a while, my Spirit-led morals always led me in the right direction. In fact, when I put Christ first, I know that I am setting an excellent example for my son. If I follow the principles of a true Christian and put Christ first in all that I do, I will be a great father and a great husband.

If you are not a Christian, this is just as easy to do. It will become the two questions that will change your life. If that person that I care about the most (child, sibling, niece, nephew, grandchild, etc.) was standing right next to me, is this something I would do? If so, is this something I want them to do someday? If you cannot answer yes to both questions, then why are you even thinking about doing it yourself?

Hope Dealer

Chapter 28:

Nichols Fourth Law and Recovery

Nichols' Fourth Law says that you should "avoid any action with an unacceptable outcome." This is about as straightforward as you can get, but it probably still needs to be broken down. Some choose not to accept anything and argue against everything. I would call them naysayers, but they don't really run around saying "nay," so I guess that title is out. I will call them fun-suckers because they have the ability to enter into any conversation and suck the fun right out of it.

In fact, here they are now...Ummmm, now...Okay, now?

"Everything can have an unacceptable outcome, so I guess this means that we should do nothing. Is that what you are telling us?"

"Yes, that is exactly what I am telling you. Do nothing, nothing at all. That shouldn't be hard, right?"

"I do nothing all the time."

"Untrue, doing nothing is impossible. I dare say you are not factually reporting. Care to argue that you do nothing?"

"I don't do anything when I sleep, so there," spoken with an outstretched tongue! Actually, you are dreaming, breathing, and your muscles are repairing themselves while you are sleeping. Just an FYI, sleeping is not "doing nothing." Sleeping is definitely doing something. So is sitting, standing, lying down, playing video games, etc. You are always using muscles, and you have neurons firing electrical impulses. Do you have anything else? I thought not."

Now it is true you can do just about anything and have a negative outcome. It is also possible that you can do just about anything and have a positive result. Case in point, I heard about a guy who took ecstasy for the first time and was hit by a semi. It was deemed the semi's fault, and the guy who took the ecstasy was awarded three million dollars. I would not recommend going out and taking ecstasy to get rich just because of that one occurrence. That is a random, chance occurrence that is highly improbable.

So, what we are talking about is likely outcomes. We mean, you should not be taking any actions that make unacceptable outcomes probable. Here are several examples:

1. I don't want to get into a bar fight. Going to bars could lead to this outcome, which I have deemed unacceptable. Therefore, I do not go to bars. "That doesn't mean you won't get into any fights, just because you don't go to bars," yells the cynic. "True," I reply, "but the fights I get into won't be bar fights. If it's in a house, it will be a house fight. If it's in the street, it will be a street fight, but there is zero probability it will be a bar fight because I do not go to bars."

2. Imagine I don't want to have a baby. I know that having sex can produce babies. In fact, it is one on a very short list of ways babies are created, and the only way for it to happen unplanned. If I have sex and I do not want

or am not ready for children, then it could produce an unacceptable outcome, so I will not have sex.

3. I don't want to go to jail. I know multiple things could cause me to go to jail. They range from murder to theft, to doing drugs, and on and on. I make sure, to the best of my ability, that I follow the law.

So, what is Nichols' Fourth Law? It is using logic and common sense to make informed, positive choices. Using rational thinking and a process of elimination and deduction, you look at the possible **likely** outcomes of an action before you engage in it. If the outcomes are acceptable, then you take action. If the probable outcomes are not acceptable, then you do not.

I used a hybrid of this with the three questions that changed my life from the previous chapter. Remember, before I would engage in something, I would ask myself these three questions:

1. If my son or daughter was standing here, would I say or do this?

2. If Jesus was standing here, would I say or do this?

3. Is this something I want my son or daughter to do?

If I could not answer yes to all three of these questions, I had no business doing it myself.

Let's use these same questions regarding drug usage. For starters, do you want your children to watch you doing drugs? Would you get high if you were standing next to Jesus? Finally, do you want your children to do drugs when they grow up? Not, will they experiment, or will they do drugs, but do you want them to? If your answer to any of these questions is no, then you should not do drugs. So, I know I should not do drugs. How do I most readily accomplish this?

Nichols' Fourth Law states that I should avoid any action that would make me doing drugs even a possibility. I know that being around people who do drugs and going to places where drugs are abundant could enable me to use drugs. Therefore, I avoid the playgrounds and playmates (defined in the next chapter) where drugs are likely to be in use. It is that simple. If I am not around drugs, they are hard for me to do. If I do not do them and my kids know I don't do them, they are less likely to use themselves. That is what I call a win-win situation.

That is why Nichols' Fourth Law is essential; it forces us to think before we act.

Chapter 29:

Playground, Playmates, and Playthings

Many things are discussed in treatment and groups such as Narcotics Anonymous, Alcoholics Anonymous, Celebrate Recovery, and SMART Recovery that will allow you to make positive lifestyle changes. Some are more important than others if we want to remain sober and advance our recovery. What I would consider to be a couple of the most important things that all of those programs talk about are your playmates, playgrounds, and playthings. I briefly made reference to this in the previous chapter. These three things can be significant obstacles and create insurmountable barriers in our environment and will keep us from making beneficial changes.

When they refer to playgrounds, they are talking about the places that you frequent. As a former therapist, I tell people they should avoid their old playgrounds. As a Christian, I tell people they may not want to frequent their old hangouts also. I tell everyone that is making changes; they need to not only be aware of where they partake of their hobbies, but also the hobbies they engage in. The hobbies they engage in are referred to as playthings.

When they mention playthings, they're talking about triggers and hobbies. Triggers are the things in our life that make us think of the habits that we are trying to rid ourselves of. Here are some examples of playthings or triggers:

1. If you are trying to work on financial issues, credit cards may be a trigger for you. Cutting up your credit cards may be a good idea for you.

2. If you're an alcoholic, fishing may be a trigger for you. In the future, you may want to only go fishing with sober people who were supportive of your sobriety.

3. If you like to fight or have anger issues, certain concerts and bars may be triggers for you. I know that they were for me. I did not stop going to concerts; instead, I began listening to worship music and going to worship concerts versus the hard rock and rap concerts that I used to frequent. I found that worship music and worship concerts tend to uplift me and fill me with hope instead of causing anger in me. I still listen to metal and rap, but the message in the lyrics is uplifting and hopeful.

4. For those who suffer from depression, isolation may be a trigger for you. It was for me. I came up with an action plan for things to do when I began to isolate, which included calling a sponsor and accountability partners. We will discuss those when we get to playmates.

5. What if you're addicted to video games? I found that a good thing to add to my life was reading the Bible, attending small groups, and actually spending quality time with my wife and my children. My family deserved so

much more of my time than I had devoted to them when I played video games.

We also need to ensure that we are aware of the places that are dangerous to overcoming the habits we are trying to change, or us living a better lifestyle. If you continue to frequent your old haunts, you are putting yourself at risk of once again engaging in behaviors you are trying to stop. Do not give relapse, sin, or the devil a foothold in your life. When we frequent places of ill repute, that is what we do.

Listed below are a couple of examples of playground situations that we may want to avoid:

1. If you are an overeater, there may be a bakery that you pass by on your way home from work that you always stop at. Would it not be wiser to change your route going home than it would be to drive by the bakery every day? Remove your object of temptation.

2. If you have a sexual addiction, why would you ever go to a bar or a club? This is the last place I would ever go to. For starters, the temptation to pick somebody up will always exist there. Most bars and clubs are nothing more than meat markets. Secondly, intoxicated people are not that much fun to hang out with if you are sober.

3. I was an alcoholic. I also enjoy playing softball. I always played softball at the fields that had bars at them. When I stopped drinking, I found a league that was played in a park that did not serve alcohol. This was a good idea because if alcohol were not available to me, I would not drink. Since there is no alcohol there, there are not typically fights like there were at the fields that serve liquor.

4. I enjoy playing pool and bowling. I am not good at either of them, but I do enjoy them. There are multiple bowling alleys in the town I live in. There are also various places

that I could play pool at. There is a Christian bowling alley in the city I live in that also has a pool table. Therefore, I can play pool and bowl in a place that has no liquor served at it. Once again, if there is no temptation, then it is less likely that I will stumble.

Do the above examples make sense? Why would you tempt fate? If I have a box of rattlesnakes, I am not going to stick my hand in there on the off chance that they might bite me. That is what we do when we frequent places we should not. We basically play Russian roulette with our new lives. The snakes are the places we go, and the snake bite is our relapse. We risk relapse every time that we enter into an environment that is a temptation to us.

The Bible supports this. In Proverbs 14:11 (NIV), it says, "The house of the wicked will be destroyed, but the tent of the upright will flourish." Why would you want to hang out in a house that you know will be destroyed? Would it not be better to hang out in a place that will flourish? I would certainly think so.

When recovery groups refer to playmates, they are literally referring to the people that we spend time with. There are people in our lives who engage in the activities that we are trying to no longer participate in. We tend to surround ourselves with people that we feel comfortable around. When I first entered into a new lifestyle, I needed to surround myself with people who will support the way that I now choose to live.

This is actually one of the most challenging things to do. We may have used drugs or alcohol with our brother, sister, husband, or wife. We may not have any friends at all that do not do drugs or drink. We may not, when we look at our lives realistically, have any true friends.

When I have someone ask me what a true friend is, I ask them a question in return, "If you had one thousand dollars on your dresser and you were leaving the house while your friend was staying there, would you hide the money before you left? Or would you be confident that the money would still be there when you come back?" Another question I ask them is, "Have you ever been in jail or prison for more than a couple of weeks? A true friend is the one who came to see you every week and always made sure there was money on your books." What most of the people I work with discover is that the people they thought were good friends are generally nothing more than acquaintances.

In my past, I had friends that would have helped me hide bodies, but they also would have helped hide my body if they could have made any money on it. The truth is, they were only my friend because they either wanted what I had, what they could get from me (because I had drugs and money), I could get rid of their drugs, did drugs with them, or because they were scared of me. It is tough to admit it, but I had very few true friends.

The following is a story that I share about finding out one of my old acquaintances was indeed a friend. I moved when I got clean. Instinctually, I knew that I could not stay clean and still live where I had been a drug dealer for so long. When I relocated to Springfield, Missouri, I worked at a local restaurant in the mall. I saw one of my old friends several times over five years. Every time that I saw him, he would catch my eye, then turn around and leave the restaurant. I was at the mall Christmas shopping when I saw my old friend again. He walked up to me and asked me how I had been doing.

"I have been doing really well, but I have to ask you a question," I replied. "How come every time I've seen you since I left Branson, you have and made eye contact with me then left the place I was at before I could say hi?"

"It was because I was still dealing drugs, and I knew that you weren't anymore. I did not want to be a temptation to you."

"So, why are you talking to me now?" I asked.

"I am talking to you now because I am no longer doing drugs. In fact, I have been off of drugs and out of that lifestyle for a year now. Unfortunately, I had old charges that came up, and I have to turn myself in to complete a federal prison sentence in January. I was actually hoping to run into you. I just wanted you to know that I got clean too."

After that, he and I talked for probably an hour about our lives and what we were doing. As I said goodbye to him, it dawned on me that he was actually a true friend. He knew that I could probably not maintain the lifestyle I was living if we were to remain friends. So instead of being a negative influence, he chose to not be in my life at all. Honestly, I had very few friends who did not do drugs when I finally got off of drugs. I had chased them all away. This was someone who actually was my friend, and because he was my friend, we could not be around each other. He thought that it would have been dangerous for me if we had even talked. Looking back, he might have been right. It may have been hazardous for me to have contact with him because the last thing I needed was the temptation.

There's a reason for that. In addiction, we tend to chase away the people who do not do drugs. We stop being friends with people who genuinely care about us because they tend to want to see us improve our lives. They remind us of the negative things that we are currently doing. So instead, we surround ourselves with people that do not have our best intentions at heart.

The Bible in 1 Corinthians 15:33 states that, "Bad company corrupts good character." And Proverbs 13:20 says, "He who walks with the wise grows wise, but a companion of fools suffers harm."

From this, we learn that it is critical to make positive friends. It is hard to learn how to be sober if we hang around with drunks. It is hard to stop committing crimes if we hang out with criminals. If we want to make changes in our lives, we have to be willing to do whatever it takes to make those changes. This includes no longer hanging out with our old playmates and beginning to hang out with new ones. Aerosmith, in their song Amazing, says it best, "I kept the right ones out and let the wrong ones in."

Do not get me wrong. I still have friends from my past who are in my life and others who are not. There are some things that I will not be around. I do not hang out with criminals, nor do I hang out with people who are doing drugs. I do not run around with people who break the law either. I believe in self-determination. I have found out that I cannot change my friends, just as other people could not change me while I was still active in my addiction. I have found the best way to be there for those types of friends is for me to live my life right.

That said, there are people from my past that I'm still friends with. For example, look at the people that I used to be friends with when I was an alcoholic. Many of them still drink. A couple of my best friends drink, yet I still will go out with them. I will meet them for dinner and a movie. After the movie is over, I will go home, and they will go to the bar. I feel that one of the best ways we can support others is by still being their friends. That does not mean we put ourselves in dangerous situations, but that doesn't we can't let people know we care and are here for them if they need us.

You may be asking yourself, where do I find new playmates? There are twelve-step recovery groups, church groups, community support groups, therapy groups, and even online support groups. These kinds of groups are essential for several reasons. For starters, we have a chance to be around people who know where we have been and can relate to us. This generally stops people from being judgmental. Secondly, we get to be around people who will share with us their strength, experience, and hope. Finally, we get to learn new behaviors from people who actually exhibit them. Proverbs 27:17 says, "As iron sharpens iron, so one man sharpens another."

When I began to hold myself accountable, I also needed to be around others who would help me be accountable. It is tough for me to make wise choices when I hang out with people who are not making those same choices themselves. If I want to begin a new lifestyle, I need to ensure that I hang out with people who also follow that lifestyle. I found the best way to do this by being around people who were where I want to be. That does not mean when I have outgrown people, that I am no longer their friend. What that does mean is that I am constantly finding new people to become friends with.

At first, I found a sponsor, who is someone who helped me work through the twelve steps, which I am a huge advocate of. They can really help you when you are working through difficult issues and trying to overcome them. In time, I traded my sponsor for a mentor because my focus was no longer on not using, but instead, it was being a better father, husband, and starting a successful nonprofit.

As you can see, changing our playmates, playgrounds, and playthings needs to happen to achieve a new way of living successfully. These are three things that are an integral part of recovering from anything that causes us harm or separates us from God.

Chapter 30:

My Platinum Rule

Most of us know the Golden Rule or ethic of reciprocity, "Do unto others as you would have them do to you." That was a quote attributed to Jesus in the New Testament. That seems great, doesn't it? It sounds so good that you can find it in just about any other religion as well:

- Judaism, "You shall love your neighbor as yourself."

- Confucianism, "Try your best to treat others as you would wish to be treated yourself."

- Hinduism, "One should not behave towards others in a way which is disagreeable to oneself."

- Islam, "Not one of you is a believer until he loves for his brother what he loves for himself."

- Jainism, "A man should wander about treating all creatures as he himself would be treated."

- Buddhism, "Hurt not others in ways that you yourself would find harmful."

I have heard these sayings in one form or another, as displayed above, multiple times throughout my life. I seldom saw it applied, so I never really took the time to think it out. It did not register with me because I knew no one would want to be treated as I thought I deserved to be. As a child who was physically and sexually abused, I always felt less than. I expected to be treated poorly and looked down on by people. I thought that was my penance for the sexual abuse that I had undergone. I was dirty and disgusting, and I deserved whatever I got because of it. I never once doubted the beatings I suffered were not deserved. I thought that I deserved to be hurt. I was an outcast.

As I grew up, I became furious and violent. The saying I heard was, "Do unto others as they would do unto you, but be first." That became my motto. In my addiction, my anger and self-loathing grew. I could only find happiness in chaos, and that was fleeting at best. I wanted to die and tried to put myself in countless situations where that would happen. I tried to kill myself and almost succeeded. I wanted people to hurt me. I wanted someone to kill me. At this point, I am sure you can see how the Golden Rule would not have been very golden for me to follow.

As I tried to step into recovery, I still believed that I deserved to be hurt. I felt that I deserved pain for all of the people that I had hurt. There was a massive trail of broken lives in the wake of the tornado my addiction had created. I was actually going to see a dominatrix when I first sobered up, not sexually, for the punishment. It helped me clear my mind when I was overwhelmed. Then the Golden Rule was reintroduced to me by my sponsor, but I still had trouble understanding it.

Next, he introduced me to the Silver Rule, thinking I could understand that better. The Silver Rule posits, "One shouldn't treat others in a way they would not like to be treated." This still did not work due to my low self-esteem and disappointment in myself. I knew that I deserved all the bad I had gotten in my life and a lot more. When bad things happened, I chalked them up to karma and me reaping what I sowed.

As I stepped into recovery, that just did not work for me. I had to become more positive, and making amends as I worked through the steps helped me, but I needed more. What I discovered was, as much as I disliked myself, I loved my sister. At the time, she was the person I loved the most. She had been there for me, loving me through all of my poor choices and bad behavior. Her love had been a great demonstration of unconditional love. I did not ever want to see someone mistreat her. Even in my addiction, I always had her back. This is where I came up with my own Platinum Rule: **Treat people the way you want them to treat the person you care about most.**

That was all it took to get me to understand the Golden Rule and apply it to my life in early recovery. When I had my son, he was added as a person I care about the most. Then I got married, and my wife was added to the list, then my daughter was added after her birth. That expanded my list and made most situations I would find myself in very easy to come up with the right answer. How did I apply my Platinum Rule? Here are a few examples:

1. Would I want someone to gossip about my sister and spread rumors about her? No! I would want them to come to her with their problems so that it could be worked out. Therefore, I try not to gossip about other people behind their backs and instead go to them when I have problems.

2. Would I want someone to beat up my son because they were told that he wronged them? No! I would want them to handle the situation like adults instead of hot-headed children. When I hear someone wrongs me, instead of hurting them as I did in the past, I try to talk to them and find out the truth of what is going on. There are always multiple sides to every situation.

3. Would I want someone to yell at my wife if they had a problem with her? No! I would want them to treat her with respect. Therefore, I don't yell at people when I have

a problem with them; instead, I calmly talk to them so we can squash the issue.

4. Would I want someone to break into my daughter's house and steal from her? No! Therefore, I do not steal from other people.

As you can see, my Platinum Rule works for just about any situation that you find yourself in. This rule has made a ton of difference in my recovery. When used correctly, it takes seconds to pause and think before you act. One deep breath and then exhale. Trust me, for a lot of us, that is a vital pause to take. I was very impulsive in my past, and I seldom made the wisest choices when I jumped right into things. In fact, 99.9% of the time, I made the absolute worst decisions. That all has changed due to me changing my thought process. Now I ask myself, "Is this how I would want someone to treat my son, my daughter, my sister, my wife?" If it isn't, then I have no business treating them that way.

As a quick disclaimer, this is not the Platinum Rule that is trademarked. This is my own Platinum Rule for recovery. The trademarked Platinum Rule says that we are to, "Treat others the way they want to be treated." That is a horrible rule, in my opinion. I work with a lot of people who are living with substance use and mental health issues. Take me, for example. If you were to have treated me how I wanted to be treated 10 years ago, you would have shot me in the head and put me out of my misery. That or you would have got me high. Bad idea, in my opinion. I definitely don't want my Platinum Rule confused with that one!

Chapter 31:

The Garbage Theory

I wondered for years, "Why me?" and it got me absolutely nowhere. I would try to escape my past by doing good things: volunteering to help my friends move, giving the panhandler money, community service, and even counseling. Yet no matter what I did, I could never come to any kind of peace with who I was, what I had done, and what had been done to me.

That question would repeat itself over and over in my head, and I never had a good answer. Was I born unlucky, did God hate me, was I the devil's special project? Why, why, why did all of these negative things happen to me? If bad things in life were garbage, I could have started a landfill at birth that would have run out of room by now. I was stuck in the victim role for years.

At some point, I discovered I was not a victim. I accepted the things that either I had done or that had been done to me as a part of life I had to go through. That said, there was still that part of me that wondered why did I have to go through it? Why me? What was the purpose of everything that had happened to me? I was stuck in the survivor role with those questions, and not having the answers fueled my drinking and increased my acting upon the other character defects that I have.

Over time I came to realize what the purpose was. I realized why I had gone through all that I had, why I had made the choices that I had made, and why I was still here when addiction has killed so many others. I call it the Garbage Theory. It is why the twelfth step is so vitally important for those who are wired like I am. It is why we not only get experience, strength, and hope from others, but we also share ours with them. We have to own our past and see it for what it is.

Imagine that everything in our past is garbage. The poor choices we make, the things that others do to us, the trouble that we get into with the legal system, etc. I mean everything that happens. We tend to not really deal with it and keep it inside of us. We are like a hoarder, and our lives become full and stressful. That is the victim stage. We have all of this inside of us, eating at us like a parasite, and we are internalizing it, giving it no opportunity to escape. We have locked the murderer inside the house with us, instead of letting him out and then locking the doors.

Once we accept what has happened to us, we externalize it. We realize that many things are beyond our control and that addiction is a disease. This allows us to throw the stuff out. We are now in the survivor role, which leaves us questioning what has happened to us. We accept that things happen, but we do not see the purpose behind it, and it takes on no meaning. There is still no purpose! The garbage we have now been able to get rid of just sits outside of us and begins to accumulate.

We now are creating a landfill that begins to mound up, and to be honest, it has no purpose other than to stink and destroy our view. We have now built a trash site, and the garbage begins to accumulate. When your everyday view overlooks a stinking landfill site, your demeanor does not improve. It causes us anxiety, depression, anger, fear, etc. We now have feelings that are overwhelming us because there is still little to no hope or positivity. Then, the magic happens!

We suddenly think of what the purpose is...LIGHTBULB moment!!! What is the use for garbage? The only one that I can think of is compost. Compost breaks down our garbage and uses it for fertilizer. What do I have to turn into compost? I am someone who has a lot of trauma or trash in my past.

I also could use that trash once ground up into compost to fertilize the lives of other people. I can use overcoming all of my past choices and tragedies to give hope and instill strength in those who are still suffering in their addictions. I can also help those who have not yet begun using drugs, alcohol, food, sex, violence, shopping, codependency, etc. as a way to cope, escape, and numb, to let them know how it can end up.

That is the positive reason for my horrific past. Just as in the healed people heal people principle, I have wisdom now that I would never have had without my history. Wisdom only comes from experiencing something, battling it, and overcoming it. Those things that I have experienced and overcame have given me vital information that I can pass onto others. I can share my strength, experience, and hope with them. I can save lives! I am like a doctor, nurse, paramedic, or firefighter, as I have been giving training from my past that enables me to help save people's lives today.

How exciting is that? To know that what you once felt guilt over, which you internalized into shame and self-loathing, now has positive power! It can enable people to make better choices. It can save lives and make families stronger. The longer I am sober, the bigger my responsibility to help others. The higher the negative coming in, the greater the positive-going out. As Einstein said, "For every action, there is an equal and opposite reaction."

For me, the action was the negative choices and negative things that others did to me. The reaction is giving my testimony and sharing how incredible my life is now. I am eternally optimistic because I have seen rock bottom and came back on top. For that, I am blessed, and I will share my story to inspire others to attain real recovery. I am in recovery from the consequences of life, and I love to share my struggles and victories with all those whom I meet. I know for me that has made all of the difference!

Chapter 32:

Spiritual Spackle

This is a theory that I developed that is the foundation of my recovery and the new life that I live today. How have I gone from my horrific past to capture an amazing life experience I am blessed to now enjoy? It is all because of this and this only. Sometimes I tell people this is the secret sauce to the wonderful life I have today. It is what I call Spiritual Spackle. It has been vitally important in my new life of recovery and the recovery of so many others that I know.

Before I get into the Spackle Theory, I want to relate a story from my substance-using days. When I was younger, I lived in a house I was buying. This was after the move to Springfield while I was in my alcohol and steroids phase, and I did not really think things through thoroughly. That will be evident by the end of this story, probably sooner. I was a full-time knucklehead!

One day my knuckle-headedness was on full display. I think that I had gotten into a verbal disagreement with my then-girlfriend, and I went outside in a huff. Once out, I figured that throwing a tantrum and hitting an inanimate object would solve everything. Obviously, that thinking was flawed, but it was the kind of thinking I did best. Mark Lundholm calls it "first-thought-wrong," and that was the thinking that I excelled at.

I walked outside, and I punched the side of my house twice. My house was older, and it had wooden siding. When I punched the siding, I put two holes in the side of my house. Obviously, this solved nothing. In actuality, it caused a much bigger problem. Instead of just being in an argument with my girlfriend, we were in an argument AND I had done structural damage to my house.

Luckily, since I was a full-time knucklehead who always acted on that first thought that was more often than not wrong, I had an incredible idea of how to fix the holes. I could patch it up! So, I went inside my house and grabbed duct tape, then brought it outside and covered the hole with multiple strips from that magical silver roll. Presto, problem solved. I no longer had two holes in my outside wall. Instead, I had the eyesore of shiny silver duct tape covering the two holes in the yellow-colored wall at my house. I did this and stepped back from the wall, thoroughly satisfied. I thought the problem was fixed.

I left the house that way for several years, holes covered with duct tape. The issues did not really present again until several years later, when I moved. I took the duct tape off the wall so I could see what it would take to fix it. You can only imagine what I found underneath! It was no longer two holes the size of my fist but was now one gigantic hole that was at least a foot of soggy and cracked wood. Worse yet was the sheetrock behind the holes. The sheetrock was mildew, mold, and water-stained from where it had gotten wet and then dried.

In short, the wall that I thought had been covered up and protected was damaged horribly. Just because I could no longer see the hole or the damage that was done does not mean that it was better, and the problem no longer existed. Instead, it had continued to be an issue that did nothing but deteriorate and get even worse. Just because I was numbed to the problem, since it was covered and unseen, did not mean it was fixed.

Now what I want you to do is imagine that the issues you have are the rain. My fist in this story is the trauma that you experience throughout your life. Finally, the outside wall of my house is representative of your soul. As traumatic things happen to you, they create holes in your soul. These holes are emotional, spiritual, and psychological in nature and are created by various traumatic experiences. These are the things that hurt you. This is how the major craters that are created in our lives occur.

We get filled with this pain, and it creates emotional and psychological stress. This stress is then turned into anger, depression, anxiety, self-sabotage, and guilt, all of which can turn into shame. Our self-esteem dwindles, and any positivity that we once had is reduced to negativity and self-loathing. I could go on and on with this description, but I will instead break it down to two words: WE HURT!

There I am, hurt. I discovered that when I hurt, all I have to do is numb myself, and things will get better, so we try to escape (insert method of escape here). Whether I am a drinker, drug user, gambler, cutter, co-dependent, have an eating disorder, mental illness, or engage in retail therapy (shopping), I can escape from my past. If I like to sleep around, save others by playing superman or woman, or I am the perfect candidate for anger management classes, I will do the same thing. I will use those things so that I can feel better about myself or numb myself to the pain I feel. I will use my method not to hurt. It may be fleeting, only lasting minutes or hours, but it will make the hurt go away for a while.

Unfortunately, this method of escaping our hurts is something that we use is a lot like the duct tape in my example above. It may cover the damage on the surface, but what is happening underneath it all? If my best friend slept with the person that I am married to, my grandfather abused me, or I was always told I was no good, do my methods of coping really fix the problem?

Of course not, at best it is a temporary solution to a problem that is sure to recur...and recur it will. The worst part of using duct tape to cover the problem is that there is the illusion that it is better. The reality is that the problem is getting worse and worse underneath. We continue to deteriorate; we continue to beat ourselves up about the past. We dwell on things that we cannot change instead of working through them. We do not allow ourselves to grieve what happened to us, because we try to act like it did not occur or that we are better.

The truth is that we never give ourselves the chance to work through our past hurts and hang-ups because we do not face them. Every time they come up; we use our preferred method of escape to avoid them. We cause ourselves untold amounts of depression and anxiety because of the traumas of our past. Numbing and ignoring it has never done anybody any good. It just mires us in the victim role, and we never reach the survivor stage, let alone advance to being a thriver.

Unfortunately, perception for us is a reality. Our reality believes that if we do not feel it, it is better. Our reality eventually learns that by using, we do not have to feel...ever. If I can stay self-medicated, I never have to feel psychological, emotional, spiritual, and sometimes even physical pain ever again. I am insulated from what others can do to me. No matter what they do, I do not have to feel it. Our reality keeps us sick and ensures that our cycle of addiction is never broken.

That false sense of reality becomes more and more distorted. It eventually reaches the point where we begin to believe that the problem is taken care of. We walk around angry, ashamed, depressed, anxiety-ridden, and begin to push away those who care about us the most.

"But I am better," we claim.

Just because we claim there is no problem does not mean the previous issues become nonexistent. If it rains and I tell you it is not water coming down on us, does that mean we won't get wet? Of course not! Just because there was duct tape on my wall did not mean the rain was not still affecting the damage that had been done, resulting in it becoming much worse. If it is covered over, that does not mean it is fixed. For us to overcome our past, we need to admit it, then address it, which will allow for the grieving process and healing to begin. Only then can we learn from it and use it to make us stronger and wiser, then grind it down and use it to help restore others.

There are three stages that we can be in due to our past trauma. The first is the victim, still stuck in the past, allowing it to hurt them constantly.

Then we have the survivor, who has accepted that the past has happened but locks it away and does not really deal with it. Both of these people will be prone to using their preferred methods of coping or escaping, which will result in an endless cycle recurring.

The victim at least acknowledges the pain, but they do not feel that they have any control or power to fix it. The survivor is like the person who has the tiger by the tail and feels like they have succeeded. At any moment, that lion can turn around and take a massive bite out of them or knock them silly with paws the size of their heads. In much the same way, there is no telling when our method of artificially coping goes from being under our control to being the primary focus of our lives.

Then, we have the thriver role. This is where we want to be. This is the person who not only accepts what happened to them but processes it and works it out. It may have been horrific and unfair, but we realize that nothing we can take, do, or say will change the facts. It happened. Instead, we use what happened to make us first stronger and wiser, but we do not stop there. We then use what happened in our lives to help others who are hurting and suffering. We give them hope by sharing our experiences and how we have grown from them.

So, what allows us to grow from our past? What do we do to fix the holes that life leaves in us? What is there that was made for that purpose? We need to find something that comforts us and fills those holes instead of just covering them up. Otherwise, we will continue to rely on our traditional methods of escape. I do not want to escape the hurt, I want to learn from it and grow. How about you? Do you want to be defeated by your past, or do you want to work through it so that you can be stronger and wiser?

I have found two things that have worked wonders for people. Some people choose to use both of them, but due to some people's belief systems, others are only able to use one, and that is just fine. A little secret here, I have found that both work just as well for people to create better lives for themselves.

The first method that I will talk about is the one that works for everyone. That would be community impact, which some people call community service or service work. I call it community impact for several reasons. For starters, many people like me have negative memories of community service. It reminds us of hours spent doing inane things because we had a judge or probation officer tell us that we had to do them. For other people, it means setting up chairs or making coffee before a community support meeting. What I am talking about is neither of those things.

For the longest time, I felt like I was part of the recovery community, but I never felt like I was part of the community I lived in. That needed to change, and here is how we change it. What I am talking about is making an impact on your community by volunteering your time, of your own volition. This means different things for different people. Here are some of the things we have done through my nonprofit, Better Life in Recovery:

1. We partner with local schools, repaint playgrounds, and pick up the schoolyards.

2. We have a stream team that keeps waterways cleaned up and does water quality monitoring.

3. We partner with other local nonprofits and help them when they need help.

4. We go into schools, colleges, conferences, churches, and communities to share our strength, experience, and hope.

5. We advocate for those who are unable to advocate for themselves.

6. We do community education and awareness events like an annual 5K Recovery Run and Recovery Day at Hammons Field (our local professional baseball affiliate).

We have found that by sharing with others and helping others who need our assistance, we can patch up the holes caused by our past. By being of service to others, we begin filling in the holes. The difference between this type of service and other recovery organizations that do service, is we are not anonymous in any way. We contact the media about the events we do. We invite people to be proud of their recovery. We are here to make it easier for people who struggle or have overcome their struggles to come forward. We are here to show our community that we are not ashamed of who we once were but instead are proud of the men and women we have become. We may have drained resources at one time, but today WE ARE RESOURCES!

The second method is the Holy Spirit. The Holy Spirit will fix those holes. Spackle is a substance that is used to repair holes and cracks in walls. The Holy Spirit is comparable to spackle. In fact, the Holy Spirit is the spiritual equivalent of spackle. What spackle can do for a wall the Holy Spirit can do for our lives! It allows us to be guided towards happiness. It gives us the comfort we never felt from our methods of escaping and numbing.

That is spiritual spackle in a nutshell. These two methods are the one huge ingredient that many people miss, either in the form of community impact work, allowing the Holy Spirit to guide them or both. It makes recovery not only possible but amazing. It takes you from being absent in your community to truly living a better life in recovery where you are vital to your community!

I hope that you can apply this law to your life. After all, it makes you think, and what could be more important than that?

Chapter 33:

The Locker Room

I am big on using analogies for one reason; people understand analogies. For those of you that enjoy sports (and those who don't), we are going to discuss our lives using a sports-themed analogy. Whether you are in long-term recovery, actively using substances, are coping with mental illness, or consider yourself normal (whatever that is), this applies to you! I believe that we all have basic needs that must be satisfied if we want to live our lives well.

"What do we need?" Glad you asked! First, realize our lives are like a game. In most games, when you lose, you start a new game. If your character dies, you get another life. When you land on "Go to Jail" you do not pass go, you do not collect $200, and you go directly to jail. But you are still sitting at the dining room table because it is a pretend jail.

This game is serious. This game is your life. In this game, when you die, they put you six feet under the topsoil. When you go to jail, you are in a five-foot by nine-foot cell, and they might keep you for a while. This game is real, it is for keeps. Most of us only get one chance at it, so let's make the most with the one life you have been given.

So how do I make the most of my life?

First, choose a team. Are you going to play for team sober or team jacked up? Will you play for team career or team unemployed? Will you be on team positive or team negative? You see what we are doing, looking at two different choices we have in life, always leading with the favorable option. We should always focus on the positives, what we want for our life, and then by applying the rest of this chapter, we can achieve it!

Now we have made a choice. Once you make that choice, you automatically have a team owner. That team owner is your Higher Power. This is where I lose half of the people who get mad. I am going to talk about a Higher Power, and the other half I will lose with the following explanation. It happens when you are too "recovery" for the Jesus people and too "Jesus" for the recovery people. Here is why I will lose the second group of people; for our purposes, a Higher Power does not have to be God. For some people, it is, but for a lot of people I have encountered, it is not.

What is a Higher Power? It is something bigger and stronger than you. When you can't, it can. Your Higher Power will give you love, forgiveness, validation, acceptance, encouragement, and hope when you are unable to provide that to yourself. I once heard someone say that a Higher Power could be anything you want, "It can be a doorknob." If you are getting all of the aforementioned things from a doorknob, you might need to go detox somewhere.

I once saw it illustrated this way in a group when I was going through my first residential treatment. A young man said that he didn't believe in a Higher Power to the counselor leading the group. The counselor asked the young man to lie on his back. After he did, he was asked to raise his entire body a foot off the floor. When he was unable to do that, the counselor asked four of the men in the group to each grab a limb and lift him. They easily did. After they sat down, he explained the lesson that could be taken from the exercise.

"Gravity is obviously a force greater than you. There is nothing, on your own, you could do to overcome it when it had you down and out. The group of men you have been in class with for the past several weeks acted as your Higher Power. You trusted them, and because of that trust, you allowed them to work in your life. What you could not do alone, you were able to do together."

We will always encounter forces greater than ourselves and need to rely on things to get us through them. Our Higher Power gives us the confidence that we can not only survive the things that consume our lives but that we will thrive after we overcome them. Once we know we have the ability, we continue to add things that will enable us to live the spectacular lives we were born to live.

Every great team has a great coach. This guy goes by various names: sponsor, mentor, coach, pastor, boss, grandfather, dad, etc. He or she needs to be someone who has attained the life I want to have eventually or has the kind of thinking I want to possess. Just like I would never want to be trained to defend myself from someone who had never been in a fight (whether in the ring or the streets), I do not want to have my coach be someone who has never experienced what I am struggling against or successful in what I am working for.

Then we have teammates, also known as accountability partners. These are positive people who encourage you and want to see you do your best. They will call you out when you are not doing your best or setting yourself up for failure. They will walk beside you and give you feedback and support when you are trying new things. They can be friends, family, co-workers, or people who attend the same church, community support meeting, or small group. They don't need to have had the same struggles or goals, all they have to do is be supportive and positive. They have to want to see you do your best and help you along that path.

Next, we have a game plan we follow. Everyone's game plans are different. For recovery, a lot of people use the twelve steps as a game plan, others use cognitive-behavioral techniques, and others use the Bible. Some people may follow the Koran or the Bhagavad Gita while others apply the things they learn while they are at practice.

Now that we have a coach, a game plan, and teammates, we need to practice (unless you are Allen Iverson). For me, practice consists of getting together a couple of times a week for coffee with an accountability partner and supporting each other as we talk about what is going well and what is not going so well.

Before each game, during halftime, and after the game, you hit the locker room. This is where you should be getting pumped up and inspired, maybe some last-minute tips. This could be your recovery support groups, your small groups, or even church or synagogue.

If you start getting frustrated or have a couple of bad plays, you call a timeout. For us, a timeout is something that helps us cope and self-regulate. It could be mindfulness exercises, prayer, meditation, yoga, etc.

And don't forget about the home field advantage! This is where the secret sauce comes in. Going into your community and doing positive things to make it better. Become a volunteer at the Boys and Girls Club, speak in schools, paint playgrounds, pick up trash in your community.

Rituals are significant to a lot of professional athletes, as well as the fans. It might be wearing the rally cap, eating a particular meal on game days, etc. For our purposes, it is finding things that support our wellness we have to do daily, weekly, and less often than weekly. For me, a gratitude list is something I have to do every morning. I wake up thirty minutes earlier than I need to and brew coffee. While it brews, I write three things I am grateful for, and then I sip my coffee and give thanks to my creator for those three things. Weekly, I have to see a movie. It is braindead downtime for me, one of the few places I ignore my phone calls, texts, and emails. Then monthly, at least, I like to take a kayak and go floating. I call the river my second church, it is so peaceful and relaxing. Figure out the rituals that work well for you!

Here is all of that in a nutshell:

1. **Team** = Is your life about sobriety or addiction? Choose now!

2. **Owner** = Your Higher Power. Something greater than you that gives hope, support, forgiveness, and validation

3. **Game Plan** = Twelve Steps/Bible: a guide for how to live your life well (Other religious texts or scientific methods like cognitive behavioral theory (CBT) may apply for you)

4. **Coach** = Sponsor/Mentor: someone living their life the way you want to live yours

5. **Teammates** = Accountability partners: people who will call you out and keep you honest

6. **Practice** = Meetings with like-minded people such as our teammates

7. **Locker Room** = Recovery Support Groups/Church: things that charge your spiritual batteries

8. **Time Out** = Prayer/Meditation: to focus and calm down

9. **Home Field Advantage** = Community service: things done altruistically for the community, making you a vital part of it. Stop taking resources and become one while working side by side with others!

10. **Rituals** = Things that you need to do daily, weekly and monthly for your wellness

These things are vital for long-term recovery. If you apply these ten things to your life while avoiding negative people and places, I guarantee that you not only can but will have a Better Life in recovery!

Chapter 34:

How Music Changed My Life

There is something about music that really affects us. It has the ability to impact our lives, it can make life livable. Even Friedrich Nietzsche had to admit that. He said that "Without music, life would be a mistake." Music is a great escape. It can save us from our feelings, or it can intensify them. Maya Angelou said, "Music was my refuge. I could crawl into the space between the notes and curl my back to loneliness."

Music has always affected me in immeasurable ways. Like food is for our physical body, I believe that music is food for our soul. It will nourish us, sustain us; in this way, we are what we eat. Junk food is seen through our physical bodies when we have too much of it. That said, if we listen to junk music, it can be seen in our actions, our words, and how we live our lives. Just like food, music has a manifestation.

I remember listening to mostly gangster rap and heavy metal when I was in my addiction. I was angry, so I listened to angry music. I was violent, and I listened to music about violence. I used copious amounts of alcohol and other drugs, so I listened to music about drug dealing and partying. I reveled in my sin, so I listened to songs about debauchery. I had extreme road rage and have punched people at red lights and stop signs for cutting me off in traffic. The music encouraged my rage and discouraged restraint.

Don't get me wrong, I take responsibility for my actions. That said, the music helped, kind of like smoking cigarettes and cancer. You may not want to get cancer, yet you smoke. You are still responsible for the choices that you made, but the cigarettes lead to an increased probability of cancer occurring. Music is the same way. I probably would have continued making negative choices in my life without the music, but the music increased the probability of me making the choices that I did.

Even after the addiction, I still kept the music, and I wondered why I stayed angry. I wondered why I still felt such a strong pull always to do the wrong thing, to make the worst possible choice in any given scenario. I think that music is just another way that the Devil can control us. I heard songs about drugs, money, threesomes, violence, murder, etc. I sang these songs, and I liked them. Try to tell me that it is not reinforcing the behaviors I am trying to leave behind me, and you will be wrong.

Why would you go to church and hear about Jesus dying to forgive us of our sins, then leave church singing songs that praise the very same sins that Jesus died to forgive us for? I thank Jesus in church for dying to forgive the very same sins that I then praise by glorifying them in the songs that I sing when I leave the church building. That is nonsensical at best and pure sin at its' worst. I believe that it sends mixed messages to those who know that we are Christian, to our family members, and especially to our children.

If we truly believe in the Bible and are trying to represent Christ, we would not sing songs that glorify sin! If you want to change your life, why would you only change one aspect of it and not change it completely? Listening to and singing the songs that I did, was just one more way for the Devil to control, gaining a foothold into what went into my mind and came out of my mouth. It was also influencing my moods, emotions, how I appeared to those around me, and how people look at Christians, especially if I am the one that they have close contact with.

As a dad, I cannot imagine hearing my son sing the lyrics that permeated my life as an addict. Why would I want my son to hear music that is diametrically opposed to how I want him to grow up? He soaks up everything, and I know that what I listened to would have a detrimental effect on him if I still listened to it--so I do not. I have made the switch to positive, mostly Christian music. I listen to secular music, but it tends to be positive and fun, not angry, and criminal. This is my choice as I want to continue to grow positively, I, therefore, input into my heart and soul only the music that helps to imprint these traits and allow me to grow.

The bottom line is, we need to change what we ingest socially, spiritually, and psychologically. There is an acronym, GIGO, that comes to mind. It stands for "garbage in garbage out." If I continue to soak my soul with music that is garbage, then that will encourage me to act in ways that produce garbage, metaphorically speaking.

I switched to positive music. I started listening to worship music, and I still get my needs filled. I used to listen to rap, metal, and everything in between, I still get to. If you like rap, try Lecrae, NF, Andy Mineo, Tedashii, Trip Lee, and Flame to get you started. If you want metal, there is Red, Thousand Foot Krutch, and Disciple. Locally there is a fantastic band called Bred 4 War. There are so many talented entertainers. Chris August is funny! Kari Jobe is amazing, as is Laura Story. Matthew West has some excellent songs, as do Mercy Me, Casting Crowns, Crowder, Zach Williams, and so many more. There are so many songs that have impacted me. Here are the first two songs that changed my life and why they are amazing.

Even before I first began listening to worship music intentionally, I heard a song from the singer/songwriter Brandon Heath that was entitled, "I'm Not Who I Was." As soon as I heard it, I adopted it as my recovery anthem. It was also my mantra as a new Christian who was recently saved. I was able to relate to this song completely. If you have never heard it, you will soon see why this was my anthem. The song starts off:

I wish you could see me now
I wish I could show you how
I'm not who I was

I could only imagine the look on the faces of the people that I used to know if they were able to see me now that I have been transformed. Much like the ugly duckling that turned into a beautiful swan, I had a very ugly lifestyle that has been changed into what I would consider a much better way to live. I am confident that most of society would agree that my life is lived better now.

If people from my past could see me now, the way that I talk and live, my life would be all that was needed to show them how different I am now. Even people from just a few years ago acknowledge the differences they see in me.

I used to be mad at you
A little on the hurt side too
But I'm not who I was

One of the significant changes that occurred impacted my anger and attitude. *I used to be mad at you* would be an understatement. I used to be angry at everybody. The positive people in my life were either preaching at me, wanting me to change, or, in my paranoia, I thought that they were trying to take advantage of me. I was not only angry, but I was also hurt. Now that I have gotten sober and saved, there have been fundamental changes that have occurred.

The reason there have been fundamental changes is that my viewpoint has changed. I realize that much of what I was angry and hurt by were often people who wanted better for me. It was not that they did not like who I was, they did not like the person I had become. Looking back, I cannot really blame them. I was not a good person, no matter how much I tried to act like it. I did token good things with my money, but my heart and my conscience were anything but good. Sugarcoating does not change what is beneath.

I found my way around
To forgiving you
Some time ago
But I never got to tell you so

I have forgiven people that I will probably never see again. They will probably never know that I was never really mad at them unless they were to read this book. It is not so much the process of me forgiving people, as it is me realizing that I was the one at fault.

I had ended friendships out of anger when I was furious at myself, or I was tired of seeing the disappointment in their eyes that I might or might not have been imagined every time that they looked at me. I often projected my own hurt and anger onto others. I was mean and hateful because I was coming down, or I had just gotten out of jail, or just got screwed over by somebody else and took it out on them. There are so many reasons.

I found us in a photograph
I saw me and I had to laugh
You know, I'm not who I was
You were there, you were right above me
And I wonder if you ever loved me
Just for who I was

I am prone to laughter when I see the 150-pound meth addict that I used to be. When I see my old pictures, I either want to laugh or cry. My addiction has, fortunately, only aged me slightly, but it changed me. I have best friends now see pictures of me from high school, and they ask who the photos are of. They are not being nice, I have changed!

I see the people who were my "friends" in my addiction, and I know that they did not love me for who I was. When I was an addict I only had friends because I had money, I had drugs, I would give them drugs for free or cheap so they could get a hustle on, I gave them a place to sleep, I would buy them food and cigarettes, I would let them take advantage of me, I had a vehicle, they wanted to sleep with me, or they wanted to sleep with my girlfriend. Never for who I was, but what was in it for them. Sad, sad, sad, but oh, so true.

When the pain came back again
Like a bitter friend
It was all that I could do
To keep myself from blaming you

Even though we make changes in our lives, we still have things that have happened in the past and things that happen today that will hurt us and cause us pain. In my past, everything was someone else's fault. I would feel pain, and it would make me strike out at others. This changed in my recovery, as when old situations would arise (new ones too), I would look at the part that I played in them. This was progress. My old friend was blame itself. Not accepting responsibility kept me sick. If I didn't do it, I could not change it. When I take responsibility, I can then make positive changes.

I reckon it's a funny thing
I figured out I can sing
Now I'm not who I was
I write about love and such
Maybe 'cause I want it so much
I'm not who I was

I was the exact opposite of this. In my addiction, I thought that I could sing. I found out in my recovery that I could not sing nearly as well as I thought I could. It was kind of embarrassing when I realized it. I had always been encouraged to sing by people who were as out of it and as fake as I was. I can carry a tune, but it is done with a voice that cracks at all the wrong places. Sobering reality!

The second part of this verse shows the difference in some of us in our addictions. I wanted no one around me when I was an addict. I would chase people away. If someone told me that they loved me, I would break up with them. If they were sick enough to love someone like me, I wanted nothing to do with them. Now, I know that I am worth loving, and I have something to offer a partner. No doubt, I am not who I was!

I was thinking maybe I
I should let you know
I am not the same
But I never did forget your name
Hello

I have a lot of people in my past that I feel I owe apologies to that I will never see again. I have not forgotten them, nor how I have wronged them. I have instead thought that living my life well and trying to help others live their lives well is the best way that I can make amends. I also hope that maybe they will read this book or see me giving my testimony and see the changes that I have made. I do not regret what I have done because it has made me who I am. That said, I have done things that were messed up and wrong. I have realized that I cannot beat myself up about the past. I cannot change the past, I can only make positive changes today. Therefore, today is where I stay.

Well the thing I find most amazing
In amazing grace
Is the chance to give it out
Maybe that's what love is all about

My favorite line of the song! Amazing grace is truly that, amazing. Grace is both unmerited favor and being given the ability to carry out the will of God. As I continued on in my recovery and in my relationship with Christ, I found that I was undeserving of the grace that I received. I surely did not deserve favor from God.

At the same time, I realized that I deemed others as unworthy of getting grace. I would look at many with animosity and would not forgive them when they wronged me.

As I grew, I found that if I were given favor by God and the ability to carry out His will, then surely that would mean I needed to forgive others and give others favor that they were undeserving of in my eyes. As I began to give others the grace that I was blessed to receive, I stopped seeing others as undeserving and gained an ability to see others for who they could be. More than that, I was introduced to the words "unconditional positive regard," which means people have value inherently, no matter who they are and what they may have done. That is what love is about, giving people the compassion, hope, and love that they deserve, and we all deserve it. This allows us to become who we were meant to be, instead of remaining who we think we are. God blessed me, and to thank Him, I should follow what He deems important. He said that love never fails! So, I share my success with others and believe that they, too, can make positive changes.

I wish you could see me now
I wish I could show you how
I'm not who I was

I guarantee that you will see one thing if you apply this book to your life, you are changed. In the end, you too will be able to sing: I'm not who I was!

Previously, I told you about Nate and Becca and how they saw me shattered, broken, and struggling, and introduced me to church. They were two Christians who greatly influenced me as they were genuine and truly walked the walk instead of just talking about it. One thing that made me uniquely comfortable about their church was the ink wall. This was a wall that you saw upon first entering the church, and it was full of pictures of various members' tattoos as well as the meaning behind those tattoos. This is definitely not something that you would expect to see in church, but it made me feel a sense of comfort. Another thing that instantly drew me in was a song called Cry Out to Jesus, by the band Third Day. This song was the perfect song for my first experience within that church. It begins:

To everyone who's lost someone they love
Long before it was their time
You feel like the days you had were not enough
when you said goodbye.

As I heard the band sing these words, tears formed in my eyes. All I could think about was my father and how I did not get to really say goodbye. I thought about the last words that I ever said to him face-to-face and how I could never take it back. I thought about all of the times that we talked, and I took it for granted. I thought about the fact that my son would never be able to meet his grandfather, my father, the man that I call Superman.

Then came the second stanza:

And to all of the people with burdens and pains
Keeping you back from your life
You believe that there's nothing and there is no one
Who can make it right.

The tears began to roll, as I thought of how miserable I was. I had tried residential and outpatient rehabilitation, psychiatrists, psychologists, counselors, Narcotics Anonymous, Alcoholics Anonymous, medications, but there was something that was missing. The only thing that I had found that worked was alcohol, sex, and violence. It took my mind off of my current and past problems and made it right for a while. But even that was only temporary, and I knew in my heart that nothing could change me, nothing could make it right. Then came the chorus:

There is hope for the helpless
Rest for the weary
Love for the broken heart
There is grace and forgiveness
Mercy and healing

He'll meet you wherever you are
Cry out to Jesus, Cry out to Jesus

I remember that I continued to cry. I was the helpless, the weary, the brokenhearted. This song could have been written about me. What could they possibly mean that there was hope, rest, love, and mercy? I could not forgive myself, so how could anyone else forgive me. They did not realize who I was, that I was an addict, that I was evil and mean and hateful and arrogant, and every other negative thing that I could possibly think of. There would never be love for me because I could not even love myself. I was an addict, a junkie, the worst of the worst. Even though I was not using any more, I was still a drunk, and I knew who I really was! Several stanzas later, God spoke to me again through music as I heard the entire congregation sing:

For the ones who can't break the addictions and chains
You try to give up but you come back again
Just remember that you're not alone in your shame
And your suffering
When you're lonely
And it feels like the whole world is falling on you
You just reach out, you just cry out to Jesus
Cry to Jesus

Wow, even me?! Even the addict was being talked about. My life was being mentioned. I kept trying to change, but no matter what I did, I was always still me. No matter how much I tried to change what I took, where I moved, who I associated with, I was still me. I was still miserable, I was worthless. In my experience, addicts weren't discussed inside of church unless when the pastor said something like, "Don't be like these people!" I had never experienced this before, and it defied my expectations of what church or Christians were like. I was lonely, I was suffering, and the whole world was crashing down on me. I was pretty sure that there was no help for me, but I had several friends that were in the church that day with me, they had a program of recovery I had never tried called Celebrate Recovery, and the band actually rocked!

Maybe there was something different about church than what I was used to. My experience gave me pause to think and re-evaluate what I had also assumed about church and Christians. Maybe I was being the judgmental one to label everyone with my own preconceived ideas about Christians and the church in general. Maybe Christians were not all judgmental and holier than thou. Perhaps I should give this church a chance. I still did not believe in God, but I felt a little better for the first time in a while. I felt accepted, I felt a little less stress, I felt a little more at ease than when I had walked in, and I liked it. Yep, I decided, I will give this a chance and see what happens! Here I sit years later, and the journey was definitely worth it. Both of these songs were truly instrumental in my still being alive today, in my being blessed with a life worth living. I went from hopeless to hope-filled. I took the road less traveled, and it has made all the difference in my life.

Hope Dealer

Chapter 35:

God is NEVER Disappointed in You

Have you ever taken a minute to really think about what it means when we say God is an eternal, omniscient, omnipotent, and omnipresent God?

God is:

1. Eternal: God has always existed. He has always been, and he will always be. There is not a time when God has not existed.

2. Omniscient: God has complete knowledge. He knows all the things that have ever been and will ever be.

3. Omnipresent: God is in all places at all times. He is always present: yesterday, today, and tomorrow!

4. Omnipotent: God is all-powerful. There is nothing that God can't accomplish, nothing he cannot do.

One day I was upset with my son over a choice he had made. Something in the house was broken, and when I asked him about it, he did not factually report (a clever way of saying he lied) what had occurred. I was very disappointed in him, and after I let him know that I put him in the corner. As he cried his little five-year-old tears, I felt horrible.

I do not like it when my son lies to me, and I wondered how many times he would be less than honest before he finally decided that telling the truth was the way to go. I started thinking about, as a parent, having the ability to stop him from lying and being able to force him to tell the truth. If I could force him always to do what I wanted, then life would be so much easier--then I thought about God.

God is omnipotent, and He really could force us to do His will. He could make us do everything He wants us to do, saying only what He wants us to say and going only where He wants us to go. I thought about having that power over my son and my daughter.

Then I thought how mind-numbing and horrible that would be. My children would be automatons, doing my bidding, and nothing else. I would never know whether it was their choice or not because they would never have an opportunity to make choices. I would rather that they choose to do the right thing on their own eventually than being forced to do it and never have the freedom to make their own choices. After all, we learn from mistakes.

God is omnipresent, which ties in with His being eternal. Because He is eternal, He has no beginning and no end. He is the literal beginning and end because he transcends both. He was here before our universe began because He created it. He is without end or beginning and is in all places, at all times at once. There is not a day where He does not exist. This means that God can see all things at all times because He is in all places at once.

God is omniscient. He knows all things that have been done in the past, and the things that will be done in the present, and being omnipresent He even knows the things that will be done in the future. If you are getting ready to do something, He knows what it is you are going to do before you even do it. God knows what you are going to do because a part of Him has already experienced you doing it.

When we combine all of these attributes into one being we call God, what does it mean for us? It means that we have a gigantic cheerleader that watches over us. God is never disappointed in the story of our life because He already knows the outcome. Let us look at a scenario to explore this a little deeper, my addiction.

When I was using, there were times that I wanted to quit. I went to rehab, and I got my family's hopes up. When I came out of rehab, I said all of the right things. I actually attained one month of sobriety following residential treatment before I relapsed, two entire months sober, and then I was using again. My family was crushed. They were disappointed and let down, frustrated, and disillusioned. Some of them lost hope in me, and my word became worthless to them. They thought I would never quit using and refused ever to get their hopes up again because they did not want to be hurt anymore.

Let's go back to my son. Imagine him not being honest with me. How frustrated could I get by his lack of honesty? I want him to tell me the truth, yet he does not. The more he misleads me, the more frustrated I become. All I want to know is, "When will he tell the truth?"

With God, these scenarios never happen. God already knows the outcome. He knew how many times I would relapse before I finally overcame my addiction. He was never disappointed in me. Instead of saying, "There is another relapse. He has relapsed three times, how many more before he wins his struggle?" God knew I had four relapses in me before I would not use again. When I think back to my third relapse, I can hear the angels cheering, "Only one more relapse, and he is ours!"

God never gets disappointed because He already knows the outcome. Sometimes the outcome is less than desirable, but He knows to expect it. I have some really good friends who have died, and if I would have known, I could have at least cherished the time I had with them. God does that, whether we cherish our time with Him or not. That is a small piece, but there is a more important message that I took from this, and one that I hope you can use as well.

God is never disappointed in you. He knows what you are going to do before you do it. He also knows the number of times you will slip and fall before you finally pledge your life to Him. Will you still slip? Of course, for all of us sin and fall short of God's glory. But when we do, we can pick ourselves up and know that God saw it coming and loves us anyway. He forgave us before we even did it because He already knew what we were going to do.

How amazing is that? **God and a myriad of angels are cheering for you in heaven right now because they are on your side. Through every victory and every defeat, they are cheering you on.**

Why? Because God already knows how your story ends!

Chapter 36:

Are You M.A.D?

Several years ago, I worked for a large company that was combining with another similar sized company. They hosted a conference so that people from both companies could have an opportunity to investigate what the other company did, networking so that we could join forces and better support each other.

We also had plenary and breakout sessions. The last plenary we had was by far the best, in my opinion. The guy was amazing. His father was a pastor, and he was a former college football coach. To say that his session was motivational would be an understatement. When I walked out of his session, I was ready to take on the world. The reason was because of a simple question, he asked us, "Are you mad?"

At first, I was unsure of how to answer that question. I thought about it, and I want you to do the same thing. Ask yourself right now, am I mad? When I thought about it at first, I answered no. I am not mad at all. Then I thought about it a little more, and I did sense the anger. I could remember the way I felt several hours before his plenary after reading an article on Facebook about substance use.

The article itself didn't make me mad. The article was about the heroin epidemic our country has (we are really in a syndemic, but that would require an entire book to detail). The article discussed the number of people in a small Missouri rural county that had overdosed in one week. The article was insightful, educational, and well written. It was the comments that followed the article that got to me. They sickened and enraged me. My five least favorite comments were the following:

1. "Who cares? Just another dead junkie."

2. "We should give heroin away for free. Once all these junkies killed themselves off, America would be a better place."

3. "Have you heard of that flakka? (Flakka is a synthetic stimulant). It is making people act crazy. Junkies should get a free GoPro camera with each dose so that we can watch them overdose for our entertainment."

4. "This is Darwin's Theory at its finest. Eventually, all of these losers will remove their DNA from the gene pool."

5. "I hate people like this, living off other people and hurting everyone that cares about them. Junkies only care about themselves. Their families are better off without them."

As I thought about it, yeah, I was mad. As I sat there and simmered, the speaker asked another question, "What are you doing about it?" If something makes you mad, what are you doing to change it? Are you just sitting at home, reading a paper or watching the news--being an armchair quarterback or are you doing something about it?

Then he pulled out the hammer. He asked us to put on the bracelets that were at each of our tables. He told us to look at our bracelets and asked if we noticed anything. I did. The word mad was written in initial form, appearing as "R U M.A.D."

He said, "Every day I wake up and ask myself, am I mad? I hope that you would do the same thing. I challenge you to do it. I want to start a movement, with this simple question, 'Are you M.A.D.?' Are you Making A Difference?"

Bam! Just like that, my mind was blown. He was not talking about being angry. Instead, he was talking about doing something about it. I was mad about a lot of situations, especially when it comes to dealing with substance use, mental health issues, stigma, and recovery. I am educating schools and communities. I am raising public awareness. I am making a difference, even though it never feels like I am doing enough.

Today, and for the rest of your life, I challenge you to ask yourself this question every day, "Am I M.A.D.?" Are you making a difference? If you are living your life to be better and help those around you become better, you are doing something right. If you are not living your life that way, you are doing something wrong.

I implore you to make a difference in someone's life!! If something angers you, use that anger as fuel to give you the passion and energy needed to make that situation different. Don't be afraid to put yourself out there and advocate for someone. Stick up for the disadvantaged, stand up to the bully when he attacks others. Don't talk about change, be the change!

MAKE A DIFFERENCE! After all, if you don't do it, who will?

Chapter 37:

P.S. An Apology to those from My Past

Recently I got out of my car to return a Redbox movie. The car next to me had its stereo pumping with no driver inside. He or she had gone in to get something, leaving their car running with the windows down and the stereo on full blast. The music coming from the stereo was some old-school chopped and screwed remix that I used to listen to back in the day. I heard it and was instantly embarrassed for the families pulling up with children due to the language and subject matter of the song. That embarrassment led me to write this apology letter for my past behavior:

To those from my past,

I am sorry. You see, pulling up beside you with my stereo blasting while I listened to music was what I did. My music was about drugs, sex, and violence. It contained the "f" bomb in a place of importance based on the frequency with which it appeared in the lyrics. I would have windows down and sit next to you at a red-light or leave my car running while I ran inside somewhere just so you and your family would have to listen. I could care less about you and yours. I didn't even care about me back then. This is one of my more minor offenses, but I apologize.

I was not a bad looking kid in school, and I took advantage of it. When we were in a relationship, I was always on the lookout for the next cute girl. I knew I was up to no good and headed for even worse things in the future, and I tried to bring you down with me. I cheated on you, used you, lied to you to get what I wanted, and treated you as unimportant compared to my friends, my drugs, and my drinking. The truth was when I met you, all I saw was a challenge and another notch on my bedpost. For all the times I dumped you for another girl, cheated on you with your friends and sisters, used you for a one-night stand, and lied to you about anything and everything, I apologize.

I was a drug user, drug dealer, alcoholic, and an all-around party guy. I would serve you extra-strong drinks to get you drunk more quickly so that the money would start rolling freer. I got you high for the first time and encouraged you to try harder drugs so that I could make money. I got you high for free when you were trying to get clean in return for your Narcotic's Anonymous key tag. I only gave you forty cents on the dollar for food stamps in trade for drugs, knowing that you had a family at home to feed. I was greedy, and the more you got high, the more I could get high and still have a pocket full of cash. I ruined your life, and for that, I am sorry.

I beat you up over money. Just because you owed me cash was no reason to hurt you. That time you tried to short me was no reason to do the damage that I did. I thought that I had to make an example, and I went way too far to do it. Finally, just because you were with that cute girl, I wanted was no reason to lay into you, but I did that too. Looking back, all I can say is I should never have been that mean to you.

I mocked you because you believed in God. I used my lack of belief and faith in God to make me feel superior to you, especially as I got older and more bitter. I was never shy to let you know how ignorant

I thought you were. I liked to poke fun at you about your fairy-tale belief and blind faith. I took pride in finding you ill-equipped to combat my agnosticism and knowledge. I tried to shake your faith, and sometimes I did. Unfortunately, that happened too often, and I do not have the words to express my regret.

I look at the carnage I left behind. I chased money, power, sex, drugs, pain--anything to escape my past. I prided myself on never hitting you because "I didn't hit girls." Yet, I would psychologically and emotionally abuse you non-stop, never realizing that my form of abuse was, in many ways, much worse than hitting you. I took food stamps from you, never caring about the starving mouths at home because you were laid off and those food stamps were all you had to feed your family. I got you high for the first time, not caring that it led down a road that ended with you going to prison. Sometimes you died, either by your own hand or someone else's, or an overdose, or a car wreck after you left the party. I guess that makes it pretty hard for me to apologize to you now, but I am sorry.

I always justified my way of living. After all, you chose to be around me. You chose to be my friend. You chose to date me. You chose to be in debt to me. It was never my fault. You should have seen me coming. How could you not know who and what I was? I never pretended to be anything other than what I was, or did I? Besides, you would have done it anyway, or would you? I could read you; I was smart, I talked fast and lived a life even faster. I made it look fun and attractive. That allowed me to talk you into doing things you generally never would have. I got you to go further than you wanted to. I helped you graduate from wine coolers to whiskey, alcohol to marijuana, marijuana to methamphetamine, and from putting it up your nose, to putting it in your veins. For that, I beg your forgiveness.

Not to make excuses, but just to explain a little about me, I had some problems. The first half of this book is basically a record of my hurts. You know about my sexual abuse, the shame, the physical abuse, abandonment. I became violent. I learned to embrace pain and not show my emotions. I learned how to hide my true feelings and only show people what I wanted them to see or sometimes just what I thought they wanted to see.

Then I found drugs and was hooked. You have read about my addiction to more--more money, more violence, more drugs, more sex, more alcohol, more fighting, more women, more crime, more partying...more, more, more. It didn't matter what it was, as long as I could temporarily escape my life or numb myself to everything around me. Nothing was ever enough.

I hated who I was. I could not stand myself, and nothing I could do changed that. I hid it, as I always have. I would never let down those walls for you. Sometimes I would tell you I was opening up, but I was lying. I was just telling you what I thought you wanted to hear, just enough to keep you in my life. My dad's suicide and separation from my son only spiraled me down farther.

In this chaos and turmoil, I found Christ, and my life was forever changed. I had tried everything else, and my life still was falling apart, so I decided to give God a chance. After running from the truth of God and actively insisting that He was not real, I'm not going to lie, it was pretty awkward at first. I did not like church because it contained Christians. I hated Christians. Christians were weak, fake, judgmental hypocrites that lived in fantasy land, and there was no way I was going to drink their Kool-aid. Then I found a group that changed my mind.

It was called Celebrate Recovery. It allowed me to work through my hurts, habits, and hang-ups while building relationships with God and the people around me. Through that program, I found a relationship with Christ. I began to build real relationships with positive people that cared about me, not what they could use me for. I learned to like who I was and realize that if not for my past, I would not be the person I am today. I had hope again. A decade of drinking that Kool-Aid and entering into recovery have gone by, and I am surer in my beliefs than I ever was before. I give my testimony often, and I wish that you could actually be there to hear it, but I digress.

I hope you know that I truly am sorry. That is why I have put it on paper for anyone and everyone to read. Words cannot accurately express the depth of my apology, as I have damaged you in unfathomable ways. I know words are not enough, especially when put to paper and not spoken. Honestly, you are many and live all over the world. Sometimes, I do not know your name, and due to head trauma plus a wild lifestyle, there are months, sometimes years of my life, I do not remember, so I would have missed some of the ways I had hurt you. I figured that writing it and including it in this was the best way to make a blanket apology for all that I have done to you.

This apology is not just to you, though. I realize you were a son, daughter, mother, father, girlfriend, boyfriend, husband, wife, sister, brother, or friend to other people, and I apologize to them as well. If it is any consolation, my days of being a soldier for Satan are over. I turned traitor and went to the other side. I have gone from dealing dope to dealing hope. Ten years ago, I decided to make my life a living amends, a dealer of hope reaching out to those who are suffering and struggling, and I have been doing it ever since.

I know that does not change what I did in the past. It cannot make the wrongs right, but it is a start. I also know this apology doesn't change everything I did to you and the people you love. Those things all happened, and I cannot take them back. I cannot change the past, only my present, and by proxy my future. That may not be enough for you. I understand you may never be able to forgive me after all that I did to you and the people you care about. That is fair, and those feelings you have are valid. That said, I hope this letter finds you doing well and living your life to the fullest.

It is my desire that someday you find it in your heart to forgive me even if you cannot forgive me today. In the broadest stretch of my imagination, you may read this, then reach out to me and let me know how you are doing. You let me know this was heard and that you don't hate me. You might even tell me you forgive me. In closing, I want to thank you for taking the time to read this, and I hope to hear from you soon.

David aka Desperado

Chapter 38:

The #HopeDealer Movement: Get Involved Today

I am a hope dealer, and you can be one too!

"What is a hope dealer," you ask?

A hope dealer is someone who has been down a rough path. Whether it was horrible things that happened to them or negative choices they made themselves, these things led to even worse choices, compounding until one day they found themselves doing things they would never have imagined and enduring evils no man or woman should have to.

I know a lot of people who have been down these rough paths, events, and choices leading them to people, places, and lifestyles they never meant to encounter. Many will continue down those roads, living a life filled with rage, hate, depression, and/or anxiety.

They will die before they find a way off of the path they are currently on.

There are many more that make it to the end of the path and start down a new one. While they walk down their newfound path, they are consumed with hate and depression. They find sleep to be fleeting because they are overcome by nightmares and unable to get over all that has befallen them. They have no idea why things have befallen them, and because of it, they are worse for the walk they have had. They may be done with their old life, but it defeated them in many ways, and they live in constant fear of it recurring or shock over all that did occur. They never get over what happened to them.

This is not the story of a hope dealer. Hope dealers do more than just survive, they thrive! A hope dealer is someone who has walked through a perilous path and makes it out alive. In the beginning, they may feel resentment, anger, depression, and fear. These are but fleeting feelings, for they have gained strength and wisdom on their journey, allowing them to work through this and emerge better, not bitter. Many make it this far, yet they do not stand among those who are dealers of hope. This is simply one more piece in the elaborate puzzle that makes up a hope dealer.

Some will start down their new road and never look back, never acknowledge, and never share that trip with anyone; others will share it only behind closed doors with a select few. They also are not hope dealers. Hope dealers realize that why they walked down the path they once did and came out on the other side was for a reason! The reason was not to ignore what happened or keep it to themselves. No, they came out on the other side so they could encourage others by sharing their stories of victory. They live to share their strength, experience and hope at all times.

Hope dealers don't just talk behind closed doors; they are loud and proud everywhere they go. Not proud of where they have been, but proud of where they are today. They realize that it is not only the people who are trying to get into recovery that need to hear their message but the people who are still using. Even more than that, sometimes it is the mother or father, son or daughter, husband or wife that needs to know there is still hope for the person they love. We are never in a location or around an audience that doesn't need to hear what we have to share. I honestly believe that everyone needs to hear the message that we hope dealers carry! Join me in living a better life in recovery and become a part of the #hopedealer movement.

If you have a story of recovery and would like to be part of the #hopedealer movement, send us a picture or two of yourself and your story or tag us and join me in spreading the message of hope and a better life in recovery!

Lightning Source UK Ltd.
Milton Keynes UK
UKHW010748090221
378442UK00001B/16